)7

To/
Jean & Pet

Thank you

Be

Tina

CW01664042

Immortality

Immortality

Tina Somers

HALEPIT
PRESS

ISBN 978-0-9555681-0-7

Printed and bound in Great Britain by
William Clowes Ltd., Beccles, Suffolk

First published in the UK in 2007 by

Halepit Press
19 Halepit Road, Great Bookham, Leatherhead, Surrey KT23 4BS

Dedicated to my two beautiful children and my wonderful family, who have sustained me through some very bleak times and always enshrouded me in love.

Acknowledgements

Excerpts taken from the song *Immortality* by the Bee Gees
Warner/Chappell Ltd
BMG Music

Front & back cover, and 'The Photo Shoot' photographs taken at The Studio by The London Portrait Company

Book produced by Amherst Publishing Ltd
Roger Wickham

Contents

PART ONE

'So this is who I am,
And this is all I know,
And I must choose to live,
For all that I can give,
The spark that makes the power grow…'

Chapter 1

The Diagnosis

AS I sit here, in the silence of the early morning, the words to the song resound in my head as they have done on numerous other occasions. They have a very different interpretation for me than that for which they were intended, but it is a song that spans the six years since my roller coaster ride began and one which has a very personal and emotional meaning for me. It's a song that I coined as my karaoke signature tune when I still lived in the marital home, and it is therefore one that is very close to my heart. So would you like to accompany me on this very bumpy roller coaster ride? Well, strap in, because here we go!

Where were you on the eve of the Millennium? It's one of those questions like 'Where were you when you heard the news that Princess Diana had died, or when John Lennon was shot?' We all remember because it was such a momentous event. The Millennium was a once in a lifetime occasion and most people therefore celebrated it in style… I certainly knew how to push the boat out as I was in hospital sipping non-alcoholic champagne, with the fireworks on the TV and the odd nurse for company! I was having a lumpectomy for breast cancer the following morning so nil champagne for me after midnight! (I always thought afterwards that alcohol would have been much more appropriate in the circumstances!).

The previous two weeks had been like a whirlwind of emotions for me and I suspect my whole family; although I had tried to keep the news from them because it was so close to Christmas and the New Year, and this should have been a joyous occasion. But families, being what they are, suspected that something was amiss so they were informed and were very supportive, as they have been ever since. I remember very vividly how the doctor relayed the bad news to me. I had attended clinic alone as I had a very young son, and not living near any immediate family, my husband had to care for him and collect my daughter from school if I was to be held up, as at this stage no-one else was aware of my situation. They always ask 'if you have someone with you', don't they? So immediately you know that it's not looking good! 'Well, I'm afraid Mrs Somers, that you have breast cancer and it is malignant…' You don't hear anything else after that.

The doctor did actually use the term 'roller coaster ride' to describe the journey that I was about to embark on and that couldn't be a more apt description (although this one, I suspected, would be far less enjoyable than the theme park variety!). So how did all this come to light? How does your whole life get thrown into turmoil like this? Do you have symptoms? Do you feel unwell? Does your partner notice anything? Are there signs? What enables you to pinpoint the reason behind your increasing lethargy? Why does everything seem like an effort? Does this explain your recent irritability and why child care becomes a chore, rather than a pleasure?

I had originally thought that the problem was in a totally different area of the body. I mean, let's face it, you have lumps and bumps everywhere, it seems, after having children! I had pursued what I thought was a stomach (or that sort of region) problem for a while, obviously to no avail. I honestly cannot remember how that moved to my breasts but there must have been an occasion when I felt a lump (amongst all the others!) that felt unusual and caused me to investigate further. What I do recall, is the various trips to the hospital where I had mammogram after mammogram – the results of which always proved inconclusive. This went on for approximately six months, until eventually it was suggested that I have a fine needle aspiration, followed by a core biopsy. These procedures were not only invasive, but caused significant discomfort, especially after the event. I remember feeling very sore and uncomfortable whilst I was ironing one day… or was that the cancer advancing?

So now I had a reason for my tiredness and other symptoms but rather wished I hadn't. I was 36 years old. Things like this happen to other people, don't they? And didn't you have to be older? Apparently not. My husband, Mark, obviously frantic with worry, requested that I call him as soon as I had any news and although it didn't really seem fitting to relay what I had just been told over the phone, I did as he requested. I recall standing in the hospital lobby, using the public phone - not the most private of situations but I didn't yet possess a mobile – tears streaming down my face (but only because the voice at the other end was so fragile), while nurses at the reception looked on, sympathetically. I don't recall driving home that day but I must've done as I do remember my husband opening the front door to me with woeful eyes, like that of a bloodhound, and giving me the longest and most emotional hug of our relationship.

Thus began my own personal roller coaster ride. I felt numb. Although I had known that this could be the possible outcome, of course you do not want to believe that it will. You want it to be a blocked duct, or a polyp at worst… something that can be removed and cured and then you can just get on with your life. I had 2 young children to care for and a husband who worshipped the ground I walked on. I had the nice house and the suburban lifestyle, the husband with the good job in London and a wealth of things to look forward to. It wasn't fair. But then life isn't, is it? At this stage, the severity of the cancer was obviously not known. We were praying that it would be in the early stages and therefore potentially curable.

So the Millennium came and passed amid the haze of non-alcoholic champagne, TV fireworks and nurses doing various observation tests. I felt very alone. I can't recall if I managed to sleep that night, I somehow doubt it – I have a very active mind and it was obviously working overtime. The next morning I was awoken (if indeed I was actually asleep in the first place) by the nurses wanting to prepare me for surgery. Those really tasteful gowns and stockings were thrust upon me and I was whipped down to theatre. The calmness of these places always surprises me as you imagine it's going to be like something out of ER! I don't recall how I felt when I came round as this was overshadowed by the next series of events, which caused the effects of this surgery to pale into insignificance.

Apparently the surgeon who performed the lumpectomy had actually had to cut through a tumour in order to remove the lump. It was therefore larger than anticipated and further surgery, in the form of a mastectomy and lymph node removal, was necessary. This was scheduled for the end of the month. I had difficulty getting my head around this one. My body was going to be mutilated. How could I cope with that? It wasn't just that I was going to lose a part of my body that worried me. It was the part that it was. This is what differentiates a woman from a man. It is what gives us our femininity. Would I still feel attractive and desirable? How would my husband react? The only surgery I had ever had before was two caesareans, which left such a small scar in an easily concealed area, and the result was so obviously worthwhile that I was unperturbed by it. This, on the other hand, was a totally different scenario.

It was the after-effects of this surgery which had a profound effect on me. When I had recovered sufficiently to leave the hospital bed, I ventured to the private en suite bathroom, where there was a ¾ length mirror. I stared tentatively at my right-side reflection in profile. Flat as a pancake! My first thoughts were that I looked and felt like a little boy. God, I hoped that reconstruction would be swift. They were not able to do this simultaneously as they were unsure of the extent of the cancer and subsequent treatment at this stage. I was experiencing a mental conflict too – how could I be so concerned about my appearance when my life was at stake? Was I just incredibly vain? Is appearance so important? I felt guilty for thinking the way that I did but the answer to both questions was ‘yes’. Society, I am afraid, particularly now, places such emphasis on our body image that I had been brainwashed, along with the majority of the female population, into thinking that I would be a lesser woman with a breast missing.

A meeting with the breast care nurse was scheduled for that afternoon (as if that was supposed to make me feel any better!). All of this was totally new to me. Unless you, or someone close to you, are actually going through it, you really are unaware of exactly what is involved. Feeling very emotional and not really taking in what is being said to you, you are advised of the different types of prosthesis available; an attempt to make you feel ‘normal’ again. Obviously, immediately after surgery the area is very tender so only the sponge variety are appropriate; but then you also need something to hold it in place and you are not yet able to wear a bra. Once you are able to do this, you can move on to the chicken fillet variety… well that would really be something to look forward to! I had had a small lump removed from my other breast as well but this had proved to be benign. Surely I should be grateful to still have one breast? I’m afraid that at the time, this did not seem like a bonus. All it did succeed in making me feel was lop-sided!

So visitors came and went, only close family really as I was not yet ready to face the world at large with my over-sized baggy jumper, which self-consciously I kept plucking at in an attempt to conceal my flat chest. God only knows why because they all knew what lurked, or rather didn’t, beneath! A few more days’ hospital stay as the drain removing all the excess fluid needed to be removed, and then you are packed off home with your little bag of goodies, and an appointment to see your consultant in 10 days time to discuss what has been found and the extent of the cancer. These 10 days seem like the longest of your life.

Back to familiarity but also reality. Fantastic to be with your family again, your husband and beautiful children in the comfort of your own home but too sore to actually contribute very much physically. There are various exercises that you are advised to do in order to regain full mobility of your arm, which again is something that you have not previously thought of. You would not want to be restricted physically. I was quite a 'fit', in inverted commas, woman – not necessarily with today's connotations – but in the true sense of the word! Ok, so I was going to do these exercises, focus on the positive. It was going to be alright. After all, positive thought gets you a long way in life. Doesn't it? My husband was great, very supportive practically but emotionally I wasn't sure how he was coping. Through all the introspectiveness of the illness, had I failed to acknowledge how he was feeling? How selfish of me.

It is not an illness that just affects the victim, you see, but the whole family. It had been a shock for him as well as me. At present we still weren't aware of the severity of it and what this would entail. We spent a great deal of time talking over the next 10 days, in an attempt to redress the balance. He assured me that the fact that I had had a breast removed did not faze him at all. I was still the same beautiful person in his eyes – (he always had worn rose-coloured glasses!). These are the types of comments that you need to hear although you do not necessarily believe them. He was just trying to reassure me, I told myself. Of course it would matter. What about the physical side of our relationship? Had he thought of that? Knowing my husband, probably not at this stage. It would not yet be high on his list of agendas. I felt very unattractive so surely this is what everyone else would think of me? There I go again – self, self, bloody self!

The day of the consultant appointment arrived and my husband did actually accompany me to this one. After what seemed like a very long wait, we were called into a small side room. My consultant, looking slightly uncomfortable, began to relay the findings to us. The cancerous tumour had been 2.5cm in size, was a grade III, which apparently is quite aggressive, and four lymph nodes were also involved. This, I felt, was not good news. The subsequent, or as they describe it in medical terms, 'adjuvant' treatment would consist of chemotherapy (AC x 4, CMF x 3), followed by chest wall radiation. The chemo was due to start in February, so my worst nightmare had been confirmed and I had a very rocky 8 months ahead of me. Well, there go my hopes for a swift reconstruction, I was going to have to live with the chicken fillet for a while yet! Not only that, but I was also going to lose my hair. I had a feeling that I may find this even more difficult than the breast removal – at least the latter was relatively easy to conceal.

More long and involved discussions between my husband and myself ensued. Obviously plans needed to be made. The children had to be told, not that they were really at an age to understand (Lauren was 6 and Chris 3), but they needed to be made aware that mummy was going to become increasingly tired and would not be able to do all the things that she usually did; and her appearance was going to change a little (not that this would worry them unduly – children are the most accepting of individuals, aren't they?). We were also going to need to arrange help with regard to child care although we wanted to ensure that their lives remained as 'normal' as possible. My husband would have to rearrange his work schedule so that he could accompany me on my numerous hospital visits (you are advised not to drive yourself and the oncology department was quite a distance from our home) and I would need help with the day-to-day chores. Not having lived in the area for that long, and having no family close by, this was not going to be easy.

After the practicalities, there follows a period of reflection. How did I really feel? What were the emotions running through my mind? The first was anger. Why, when I had pursued it for months, had I now been told that I had probably had cancer for 2 years? If they had found it earlier, would it not have reached my lymph nodes? The second was sadness, not particularly for myself, but for the whole situation and how this would affect others. I never actually thought 'why me?' because why anybody? Why children who haven't yet experienced life? But I did think 'why now?' We were happy, having moved to the coast a couple of years earlier, to a house that I had chosen – so spacious and easy to manage. Our children were settled and it was lovely in the summer to just walk down to the beach after school – a totally different way of life to the busy lifestyle in Surrey. Admittedly, my husband had a long journey to and from work, but didn't the advantages far outweigh the disadvantages? And after all, he could relax and unwind on the train journey home, couldn't he?

Strangely enough, I did not think seriously in terms of my own mortality at this stage, I was convinced I would beat it. Because you see the world through your own eyes, you cannot imagine a world without you in it. You know that it carries on regardless, as you see this when you lose people around you. Everything, and everyone it seems, moves on and no one, it appears, is indispensable. But it did make me question, or should I say explore, my faith. I am not a particularly religious person but I do believe in a greater being or existence than us mere mortals, and we all live in hope that there is a pot of gold at the end of this rainbow. We are all striving for immortality. There must be something else, something better, surely? Isn't this just a practice run? I believe we are here to make mistakes and learn from them in preparation for what is to come. In some instances though, it would seem that we are here to suffer unfortunately, but perhaps also to overcome obstacles and succeed in the face of adversity.

Chapter 2

The Treatment

SO NOW I had an 8-inch diagonal scar where my breast once was, a chicken fillet in my specially adapted bra (they have pockets sewn into them to hold the prosthesis in place) and 7 months of chemo, followed by 5 weeks radiotherapy to look forward to. I told you I knew how to enjoy myself! I had been offered the cold cap during the first course of chemo as this was obviously the one resulting in hair loss. I decided to give this a go as anything that could prevent this had to be worth a try. The start date was looming and I was feeling a little apprehensive… not really scared, it's just that 'fear of the unknown' feeling; you really don't know what you're letting yourself in for (however much you are told) because the experience is so unique for each individual. All I knew was that the treatment would make me very tired over time, that hair loss and nausea were likely to be other side effects and that I would need help with running the house and more importantly, with the children.

My husband, Mark, as I mentioned earlier, is very good at dealing with practicalities, he does this every day at work in his capacity as Project Manager. He had worked for the same employer since leaving school so was well known to the company and thankfully they were very understanding (in fact, they sent me the largest and most beautiful bouquet of flowers I had ever received, in sympathy for my situation). He was therefore able to rearrange his workload to a certain extent, which in turn enabled him to accompany me to the hospital for each chemotherapy session. It was arranged that my parents would come to stay for 3 days a week during the treatment to assist with the children. Fortunately they were retired. It would have been very difficult had they not been as they lived a fair distance from us. They were a tremendous help and quite frankly, I don't know how we would have managed without them.

There was one other appointment I needed to make before the treatment commenced – the hairdressers. You see, I had long, straight hair, which I was very proud of because it was very shiny and healthy looking (someone once jokingly asked me if I polished it!) but the majority of it was possibly going to fall out so I felt it would be easier to have it cut short before the treatment began – you are advised to do this anyway. I actually went to a hairdressers near my parents as I didn't want to have to explain my actions, I wanted to be anonymous. As the hairdresser made a pony tail and then snipped the whole lot off in one go, I gulped and suddenly a great sadness came over me. It wasn't just because of the haircut. I think the reality of the situation was dawning on me for the first time. Until now it had all been talk and speculation but now I realised that it was actually happening because I was physically doing something in preparation for it. I walked back to my parent's home in tears. I wished afterwards that I had had more foresight as I would have taken the hair with me. It would perhaps have come in very handy later!

I was, in fact, offered a wig and I did go for a fitting at the hospital. But because I normally have very fine hair (although lots of it), the wigs all looked ridiculous on me; they were twice the volume being made of synthetic, rather than natural material. I did contemplate buying one privately, or having one made but they are so expensive and if the hair loss was going to be both temporary and partial, I decided to make do without; after all I didn't want to look like I had a dead cat on my head, did I?! For these reasons I couldn't justify the cost of having one made at this stage, and I'm not actually sure that I wanted to… some of them put me in mind of a Benny Hill sketch – maybe it was just the way I was wearing them! Others reminded me of a Murder Mystery evening at my in-laws, when my mother-in-law had donned a wig for her role, which was a great source of amusement as it kept slipping off, or her head would move but the wig didn't come with it! Head scarves therefore seemed the sensible option so that's what I chose.

The day of the first chemotherapy treatment arrived. The first step was to have the cold cap fitted. This is rather like a frozen riding hat! It is the most extraordinary feeling having your head turn into a giant ice lolly! After a while it becomes very uncomfortable, the pressure on my temples was enormous. Still, if it was going to prevent some of my hair falling out, who was I to complain! You then have the chemo with the cold cap in place. This is also an unpleasant experience. They insert a cannula into your arm, then attach the drip full of the chemo solution. This then infuses into your vein over the next hour and a half or so. I was in a room with other women undergoing the same treatment – one in particular springs to mind. She cannot have been more than 20 years old and was accompanied by, who I assumed, was her mother. I felt a huge pang of sympathy for her… she was so young. She still had her whole life, including child bearing years, ahead of her. At least I had been fortunate to have already experienced that privilege.

After the first treatment, I didn't feel too bad but as I understood it, it was the cumulative effect of the treatment that eventually would take its toll. I think it was after the second treatment that I started losing my hair. Even though you know it is going to happen, it is still a shock. It was coming out in small handfuls, and not just from my head! I remember calling Mark in from the garden and showing him. It was actually quite fascinating at first as I still had a lot remaining but as time went on, it ceased being so and became a nuisance as apart from anything else, it's messy… you find hair everywhere.

As the course of treatment progressed so did the symptoms. I did experience all the side effects they had mentioned in varying degrees. I still had some hair, just enough to poke out the sides of my headscarves but I was grateful for small mercies! I was still functioning, that was the main thing. I attended the children's sports day as usual, celebrated their birthdays with them, and tried as much as possible to carry on with normal life. As I progressed to the second course of treatment, I was feeling more tired and low. I think it was this one that made my skin turn a nice shade of tomato! I remember one of Lauren's friends saying to her that 'her mummy wore far too much blusher!' I actually felt, and probably looked, like a Belisha beacon!

We had come into some money through a Critical Illness scheme that we had contributed to so we decided to have some work done on the house and garden. I was obviously there to oversee the work and we had a very nice decorator, who commented on my wearing 'those silly scarves' as he put it! I really don't think he realised what was going on as we never discussed it, although I would have thought it was obvious. Further on in the treatment, he told me to stop cleaning and have a rest from time to time, or go shopping with a friend. I wasn't sure whether he was trying to get rid of me, or whether he felt sorry for me as I spent a great deal of my time indoors. He once said 'you're not going to collapse on me, are you?' By Jove, I think he'd finally got it!

The treatment was by now becoming quite gruelling. My veins had always been difficult but now they were distinctly elusive! It was decided that I should have a PICC line inserted, which would make administering the drugs easier. This is a tube fixed permanently under the skin, with an opening on the surface for easy access. Unfortunately my body didn't take too kindly to this type of invasion. It became infected and had to be removed, so it was back to being a pin cushion again! My blood count had become so low that I was unable to have chemo that month so it was prolonged for a further month. Even my consultant was worried. I recall feeling so weak at one stage that I could not even manage to make a cup of coffee. Instead I rested my head on the kitchen surface until my mum rescued me and took me up to bed. I think your body has a way of telling you when enough is enough.

Throughout the duration of the treatment, Mark worked

as usual. Not getting home until after 8 most evenings. Occasionally he worked from home. The three days that my parents were there were relatively easy. The others, when I was alone, became increasingly difficult. I had one good friend in the area, Kirstie, who used to do the school runs and regularly have the kids for tea, which was a great help. She was in fact the first person I told after my immediate family. I remember the occasion vividly. I had taken Chris into school and bumped into her. Someone had already commented on my washed out appearance, 'your eyes!' they had said. They were obviously puffy and red, through sheer fatigue and worry. She could see that something was obviously very wrong and asked me outright. Needless to say she was shocked and upset. I came to rely on her during the entire treatment; she was the only person outside my family who consistently helped me at that time.

Mark's behaviour was a little surprising at times. Instead of coming home from work and taking over the child care, he used to go into the dining room and work on his computer all evening – even when my parents were there. Perhaps he couldn't cope with what was happening and just wanted to escape by throwing himself into something, I'm not sure. But to be honest my parents weren't getting any younger and our children were hard work for them. They could have done with a break. He was good at the weekends though, taking them off swimming or some other activity to give me some peace. The kids were the same as ever, constantly arguing and testing the boundaries. When they were reminded, they would try to be very good but this was usually short-lived and they would, of course, revert back to themselves! They didn't really take much notice of my hair loss and change of appearance, they just took it all in their stride. Fortunately, they were unaware of the seriousness of what was happening. Thank goodness for that.

By the end of the second course of treatment, the hair that I had lost was starting to grow back, and I visited my local hairdresser to have it tidied up as it obviously doesn't all grow back at the same rate. She worked from home, which made it an easier and less daunting prospect. She was also aware of my situation and very understanding although I still think she was a little shocked when I removed my scarf. I kept wearing my scarves until my hair was long enough to be considered 'a style'. I even wore them on our summer holiday to the South of France as this is how I felt comfortable.

The other thing that you don't think about until you are in this position, is that you have to buy your bras and beachwear at a specialist shop. Fortunately, there was one quite locally, which made trying on easier. The choice however, was very limited and it was difficult to get, a) something fashionable, and b) that hid any discrepancies between the prosthesis and your natural breast. Not only that, but the majority were more expensive than high street stores, which I actually think is unforgivable. It seemed like these companies were benefiting from others' misfortunes.

I always disliked visiting this shop as although the assistants are very well-meaning, they hover around you to see if they can assist in any way. Being a very private person, I prefer to be left alone. But I would be in the middle of removing the prosthesis from my bra to place it in the swimsuit and the curtain would quiver. 'Are you ok in there? Need any help?' 'No, no, I'm fine thanks!' I'd utter through gritted teeth, trying to get the prosthesis in place as quickly as possible so that if she did enter, she wouldn't see too much! It wasn't that I was ashamed of what had happened to me, it's just that I hadn't come to terms with it yet… I never have if I'm honest. I should perhaps be grateful that there are these type of shops. Years ago, you would just have had to make do with whatever you could to disguise your missing breast. That's if you'd survived in the first place. But because I'm a perfectionist and had a relatively good figure before all this, I felt that it was unsightly, that it looked unnatural and I therefore did not want to be appearing in anybody's freak show.

Although I felt very self-conscious wearing my specialised swimsuit, I did sit around the pool with the rest of my family on holiday but I would not go in the water, even though it was stiflingly hot. I was just too concerned that someone would notice, or that my prosthesis would become dislodged and float to the surface. When we visited the aqua park, I could not bring myself to go down the water chutes for the same reason. I also, funnily enough, felt a bit of a fraud; I was hiding something, like a hushed secret.

I wish I could have just accepted it but I'm afraid that being who I am, this was not possible. I have never willingly shown anyone the scar, not even my husband, as I could not accept that this was who I now was. I felt like a completely different person. In spite of that, it was a lovely holiday. My mother-in-law and nephew joined us for part of it and they were great fun. They also helped keep the children entertained so that Mark and I could have an evening or two to ourselves. But all good things must end and I had a five week course of radiotherapy to return to.

Chris was starting school that September. I had told the teachers about our situation as I thought they needed to know so they would understand if the children were upset or unsettled at all. They were very good about it and Chris's teacher agreed to take him full-time from September, rather than December, to allow me to get through the radiotherapy with as much ease as possible and to aid my recovery. Although it was very kind and helpful of the school to make this exception, I now hugely regret that decision as I wish I had had the time with Chris instead. You can never replace that, can you? The time when your children are little and their entire universe centres round you. You cannot get the time back and they grow up so fast, especially these days, don't they? Then they don't appear to need you as much.

I had decided to take myself to the radiotherapy sessions. The holiday had refreshed me and I had recovered a little from the chemo. I felt that radiotherapy couldn't possibly be worse than that anyway! This was true. I had a five minute slot at the same time each day, with weekends off for good behaviour! The car journey however was forty minutes each way, and as they were often behind schedule it took a sizeable chunk out of my day. The treatment consisted of radiation being directed at the treated area, in an attempt to kill off any lingering cancer cells. I didn't experience many side effects from this treatment – it wasn't even particularly sore although I did wonder whether this was because of the scar tissue; the area felt quite numb after the surgery. Towards the end, there was a little discomfort and redness but on the whole, my body coped with it really well, apart from the obvious tiredness.

Once the treatment was over, they had to decide which

medication to put me on to keep the cancer at bay. It was decided that because my type of cancer had a hormonal element to it, it would be receptive to a drug called Tamoxifen. I would also have to have Zoladex injections at four-weekly intervals which would further reduce the amount of oestrogen in my body. These were administered to my stomach. The side effects were hot flushes, perspiring, and cessation of menstruation (not to mention increased facial hair!); it was basically a drug-induced menopause. This was recommended for two years. So, although I had lost a breast and undergone months of treatment, I wasn't at the end by any means… far from it. It was going to be an on-going saga. I have to say that it felt very ageing to be having menopausal symptoms at such a young age, but it was apparently prolonging my life – a minor detail!

Having seen me go through so much, my husband wanted to do something nice for me – to give me a treat. He knew how much of a sun worshipper I was and it was October now, it was chilly and the nights were drawing in. Without my knowledge, he booked and paid for a holiday for me and my closest friend, Jenny, to go to Faliraki, Rhodes. He had been the one who told her about my illness in the first place as I had not been in contact with her for a while and didn't know how to break the news to her myself. Cowardly, I know! Between them they had secretly arranged this and Mark had again rescheduled his workload so that he could look after the children while I was away. What a really kind and thoughtful gesture. I knew nothing about it until the last minute and was delighted… this holiday was however to change my life and unfortunately, Mark's complete kindness was about to backfire on him.

Chapter 3

The 3 R's
Recovery/Remission/Reconstruction

SO I met Jenny at Gatwick as planned. Mark and the children came to see me off. I think Jenny was a little shocked at my appearance. She hadn't seen me for quite a while and I was thinner, tired and more gaunt-looking; testament to what I had been through. It was lovely to see her but I wasn't looking forward to the holiday perhaps as much as I should have been. It was the longest I had ever been away from the kids and I knew I would miss them terribly.

I also knew that Faliraki was known to be a 'party place' and I didn't know whether I was up to it! But I realised that I should enter into the spirit of the thing for everyone's sake. After all I didn't have to party, I could just relax, enjoy the sunshine and Jenny's company, couldn't I? (...as if! You see, I've always been a bit of a party animal and I sure as hell was not going to let my illness get in the way of us enjoying ourselves!). Having said that, it was the last week of the season so I knew that it would be quieter than in peak months – probably just as well, I don't think I could have coped with that!

Jenny is my oldest and dearest friend… still. We have known each other for over 30 years. She is the sort of friend with whom you always feel comfortable and know that she would never betray your confidences, or judge you. I think most of us have a friend like that. I really believe that there is no substitute for the longevity of a relationship.

So after the cuddles and farewells to our other halves and kids, our holiday began… we checked in and then headed straight for the airport bar (that's what Jen and I do best!). We only had a couple and then boarded the plane. It was a good flight, followed by a relatively short coach ride to our destination, which was a small complex on the outskirts of Faliraki town. The apartment was pretty basic but it had everything we needed and was basically clean. Jen and I went for a little stroll to see what facilities there were. Outside, there was a very inviting pool and a bar, which provided food as well as drinks. Two things I noticed almost immediately were a) how quiet it was, and b) that there was a massive power cable over the pool! (This would never be allowed in the UK!).

Our days were spent lazing round the pool, or occasionally on the beach. The weather was great although it did become a little chilly in the evenings. On one occasion, Jen and I decided to have lunch at a beach bar. We sat there for hours, drinking beer and discussing every topic under the sun, including Princess Diana's death and the effect it would have on her children and the world. For me it was one of the most memorable days of the holiday. Others that come to mind are our trips to Lindos and Rhodes Town, and a rather amusing incident with a hammock by the side of the pool! We had made a couple of young friends (who probably belonged in Faliraki a little more than we did!) and our day in Lindos was spent with them. After an invigorating boat trip, we lunched at a restaurant on the cliff top overlooking Lindos bay and the view was beautiful. Rhodes town was where Jen and I consumed a rather messy lunch of unpeeled prawns, and the hammock incident conjures up pictures of my numerous attempts at trying to get out of the damn thing! Not a pretty sight!

Most evenings were spent in the many bars and restaurants in or around the infamous Bar Street! There was one bar that seemed more lively than the others, which attracted us most nights. It was here that we did our partying, which included dancing on podiums, benches and the bar! Falling off any of these was a distinct possibility as apart from the fact that we had all consumed copious amounts of alcohol, the surfaces were very slippery from spilt drinks. Jenny, unfortunately, was one of the casualties (although luckily, she didn't do herself any serious damage!).

This bar was also where events occurred, which were ultimately to change my life. I was learning how to enjoy myself again and regaining confidence in my appearance, due to the male attention I was receiving. There was one guy, in particular, who I was very keen on. Nothing much happened, we just chatted when he wasn't busy (he was a bar man). But it made me question my relationship with my husband and assess and evaluate my life at home. Jenny and I sat up until 4.30 in the morning discussing this.

You see, my relationship with Mark had always been a little one-sided. I loved him, of course, but for me there had never been any passion or excitement. It was just safe.

I wasn't as physically attracted to him as he was to me, and this caused problems in our relationship from time to time. I thought that we would be able to resolve this but the illness made it even more difficult. Funnily enough I met him in Ibiza, my first holiday abroad. I was with Jenny and he was with a group of friends. I just thought he seemed like a really nice guy but he was not the type I usually went for and even at this early stage, I was not sure if I fancied him. As I got to know him though, he became more and more attractive because we were compatible in so many other ways and he was (still is) a lovely man, despite his faults. He went home a few days before me and actually called me in the hotel room so he was obviously keen! I wasn't as confident as I outwardly appeared and was flattered. It was a holiday romance that lasted.

In Faliraki I was occasionally reminded of my illness and that I should perhaps be partying slightly less. There was one occasion when Jen and I were supposed to be having a 'quiet night'. We went into town as usual but agreed that we would just have a meal, a liqueur or two, and then hit the sack rather than going on to our usual haunt. This we did but you forget how large the shots are abroad and my two Grand Marniers were probably more like four! They went straight to my head and back at the apartment I went out on to the balcony for some air. I knelt down as I was feeling rather squiffy but unfortunately was not able to get back up! Jen was, by this time, tucked up in bed so I stayed where I was, trying not to disturb her. I ended up on all fours just waiting for the feeling to pass. Eventually it did and I was able to scrabble into bed.

Jen was completely unaware of all this at the time but

the next morning when I enlightened her she was mortified. I think she felt a bit guilty about it 'Why didn't you wake me up?' she cried. It wasn't her fault, bless her, after all it's me who drank the liqueurs, I should have known better! Anyway, I wanted her to have her beauty sleep (not that she needed it!). Another occasion was on the flight home, my breathing felt a little laboured and I wasn't feeling too great. The partying had finally caught up with me! But I wouldn't have changed it for the world. We had had a brilliant time, despite missing the kids and now I was just looking forward to seeing them.

Before this though, I was to have an unusual experience on the plane. It had only ever happened once before in my life. I was half dozing when I felt something, or someone, brush my cheek. I opened my eyes to find nothing there. It was one of those spooky moments when you think you're either going mad, or indulged in too much alcohol consumption! Perhaps I had just imagined it. The first occasion that I had had a similar experience, was when Mark and I went back to Ibiza together shortly after we met. We had a power cut and Mark left the apartment to find out what was going on. Left alone in the dark with a couple of candles for company, I felt a tap on my shoulder. I turned round to speak to who I thought was Mark returning... there was nobody there. Was I just hallucinating, or was there someone with me? I guess I'll never know but it really felt like I wasn't alone. Was someone watching over me I wonder?

Back on English soil, it was lovely to see the beaming faces of my two children. Mark looked tired and a little stressed, it must've been hard work for him coping with the children on his own but he was really pleased to see me looking so well, and felt like the objective had been achieved. I told him about the holiday (obviously omitting a few minor details!) and was genuinely pleased to be home with my family. However, over the ensuing weeks I could not get the holiday, or the bar man out of my mind. Every time Spiller's 'And if this ain't love…', or Mojo's 'Lady' came on the radio, I was right back there in Faliraki! I have always been a bit of a dreamer, trying to escape the banality of life. Mark and I had talked about moving abroad on several occasions but deep down I think he was loathed to give up his job, which he enjoyed and felt comfortable with. After all it was not just a job but a career, so why should he? For me however, being back in grey, chilly England was not my idea of a good time!

Gradually I began to realise that I had a life and responsibilities here so I tried to get on with it and settle back into day-to-day life. Mark noticed that something had happened to change me while I had been away, by the look in my eyes. I think he was starting to feel a little insecure. I tried to reassure him but deep down I knew that things were about to change dramatically. The new course of drugs also appeared to be having an effect on my mood and I was beginning to feel like a different person. I think the holiday had made me realise that I was still an attractive and desirable woman, despite what had happened to me, and that there was a life and fun to be had outside of my marriage. At this stage, however, I pushed the thought to the back of my mind. I had the children to concentrate on and as time went on the memory of the holiday began to fade… although the feelings never did.

Christmas came and went with the usual visits to family and friends (including the sticking of the tags on the forehead by my father-in-law!) and in the New Year (which was better celebrated than the last one!), we began to discuss our family holiday. We decided that we were going to go away at Easter, using some of the Critical Illness money and I think the intention was to make it a family holiday of a lifetime. We chose an all-inclusive holiday to The Dominican Republic, which really gave us something to look forward to. It soon came round and it was the most beautiful resort. We had an apartment overlooking the sea so that we could sit outside and watch the sunset. The kids were fully entertained by amongst other things, the huge pools and pool bar, plus the restaurant where you could help yourself to as much as you wanted whenever you wanted – the children's idea of paradise!

We stroked dolphins, fed the family of ducks who followed us around (much to the children's amusement and fascination; the ducklings were so cute!) went parascending, I did keep fit in the pool and Mark and I had the usual table tennis tournament. I still felt a little self-conscious in my swimsuit, particularly during the keep fit sessions when I wore a t-shirt as well, but I was learning to cope with it better. The evening entertainment was very good too – live shows and the hotel dance, where you could go up on stage and join in. We actually bought the CD so that we would be reminded of the holiday and could teach Lauren and my friends the dance at home… sad but true! Then there were the beautiful sunsets of course, but despite all the great features of the holiday, I couldn't help feeling that I may not be sharing these with the right person.

Back home, the holiday had further convinced me that I would really like to live in a different climate. I didn't want the busy, stressful life that most of my family and friends had. With my health problems too, I felt I needed to take it easy, and abroad this was so much easier to do. I have always loved the feeling of the sun on my face and the laid back lifestyle of Mediterranean countries; plus the diet is considered beneficial to cancer sufferers. I am one of those people who get SAD (Seasonal Affective Disorder) in the winter months and need the sunshine to give me a boost. Not only that, but I am prone to depression, often hormonally based – I had severe post-natal depression after the birth of my first child Lauren, being hospitalised for 3½ weeks. I always feel so much better and healthier in the summer, but there wasn't just myself to consider; obviously my husband needed to work and the children's schooling was important. We had talked about running a bar in Cyprus, or somewhere similar, but again that's all it was… talk.

It was my dad's 70th and my sister's 40th birthday that year and they had decided to have a joint celebration. We wanted to mark this occasion by having a full family photograph done. I'm glad we did as it is the only one in existence. It was a lovely day and, in fact, the last time that we were all together as a family. I still looked slightly jaded in the photo, but now I was starting to look and feel better day by day; the treatment was obviously working. I joined the local leisure centre and began to attend the gym and keep fit classes 3 or 4 times a week. I was getting in really good shape. I totally renewed my wardrobe as some of my previous outfits were distinctly frumpy! (It's funny how when you have young children, you tend to totally neglect yourself, isn't it? Still, I suppose you have neither the time, nor the money, to be bothering with your own appearance). I couldn't believe some of the things I had worn! Every last penny seemed to get used up just on living. But now that we had some spare cash, I felt justified in treating myself.

Since we had had such a grand holiday at Easter, we decided to have a more subdued one in the summer holidays. We wanted to treat my parents by way of a thank you for all their help and they do not go abroad, so we plumped for a caravan on the Isle of Wight, which is one of their favourite places. We were very fortunate as the weather was good and we were able to make the most of it. With my new found confidence, I even did karaoke, alone and with my daughter, much to my husband's surprise – I haven't sung on a stage since my parent's 25th anniversary when it went a bit pear-shaped! Actually I really enjoyed myself! All in all, it was a lovely break. We didn't live in each others' pockets, going off and doing our own thing from time to time. However, I could sense Mark and I were drifting farther and farther apart. I'm afraid his advances were not well-received and I gave the excuse that we were in such a confined space, being in a caravan, that we had no privacy. I think that this was the beginning of the end for our relationship although at the time, neither of us knew it.

Throughout all of this, I yearned for my reconstruction. Maybe this would make a difference both to my physical and mental state? Ever since my mastectomy, I have dreamt of having my breast restored to its former glory. I did not feel either whole, or myself, with a breast missing. This was not the Tina that I recognised. I did a lot of keep fit and loved sun bathing so I felt very restricted having to wear specialised items of clothing. Not only that but I found myself holding on to my keep fit top during classes so that no one would notice that I didn't have a cleavage; and when lying down on the beach or wherever, I would fold my arm over my chest so that you hopefully could not tell that one breast had moved with gravity, and the other (prosthesis) had stayed firmly perched on the top of my chest! Luckily my husband was with PPP so I could have it done privately. This made no difference to the quality of the surgery but it did speed the process up.

When we finally got a date, I remember feeling very excited. Was this going to be the end of feeling inadequate and unattractive? Would I get my feminine curves back? I knew that there were limitations to what could be achieved during surgery but anything had to be an improvement on a flat chest! Initially, I had wanted the procedure whereby a flap of muscle is taken from the back to replace the missing breast tissue; but because this was quite an invasive procedure, and the surgeon felt that a similar result could be achieved with less intrusion, it was decided that I would have an implant inserted that could be inflated with saline solution over time, via a port on the surface of my skin. This was chosen because the area was so taut from the radiation that it needed to be stretched into shape gradually. I knew therefore that I was not going to wake up from the anaesthetic to find a sizeable mound on my chest, but it was a start.

This was performed, and once the scar (they had re-opened the original mastectomy one) had healed sufficiently, they began the pumping up process. It was a long and drawn-out procedure and there were no dramatic results. In fact it got to the stage where the skin would stretch no more and it was nowhere near the volume of my other breast. Plus the fact that it was not going to look natural anyway as the implant was filling up evenly, rather than more liquid at the base, so it was looking more like a poached egg (minus the yoke) than a breast! The surgeons therefore had to think again. They came up with the solution that a better option may be to have a shaped implant, already with more volume at the base. I agreed with this and the surgery went ahead. I was no longer covered by PPP as they only agree to assist with one attempt at reconstruction, so this time I had to wait my turn.

When I awoke from this surgery, I was profoundly disappointed. They still had not managed to achieve the same volume as my own breast, and again it did not appear to be a natural shape. What made it worse was that the surgeon was actually pleased with the results. They were not able to re-open the original scar so a new but smaller incision was made below it. Unfortunately, like when you squeeze a bar of soap, the volume still wanted to stay in the top region so there was still no symmetry between the natural and reconstructed breast. To make matters worse, it became infected (I told you my body does not take kindly to intruders!). I began vomiting and had a really high temperature so had to be re-admitted to hospital where the infection was controlled. After all that, I ended up with a bit of a cleavage and not a lot else! But I really thought that my body had been through enough for the time being so decided to put any further attempts on hold.

PART TWO

'And I will stand for my dream if I can,
Symbol of my faith in who I am…
And I must follow on the road that lies ahead,
And I won't let my heart control my head…'?

Chapter 4

The Wayward Era

I HAD been going out more and more with my friends as I felt I had missed out in the past. Up until recently, I really had been a stay-at-home mum. However, I now felt like I needed to escape… just for a while. Unfortunately though, the group of friends I was escaping with were not liked by my husband. They were considered a bad influence. I always have liked a drink, but I was drinking a lot more now and staying out late, returning to my poor husband, in bed but awake, waiting for me. He was becoming suspicious about where I had been as I had only recently acquired a mobile phone and was receiving text messages at strange hours. They were genuinely from friends at this stage but I could see that they were troubling Mark. In actual fact, I think he was a little surprised when I had asked for a mobile phone as he probably thought 'what does she need one of those for, she hardly goes anywhere!' Little did he know that I had plans to change all that. After all, he was often out or away, and what's good for the goose…

I don't know whether I was having an early mid-life crisis brought on by my drug-induced menopause, or whether I was just disillusioned with married life and was looking for the excitement that was lacking, but I started to go to nightclubs and was getting chatted up on a regular basis by some very young men! More to the point, some very good-looking young men! I didn't go there, but this was a real ego boost as you can imagine and I was enjoying the attention. I love to dance, always have, but my style of dancing was changing – even my father-in-law noticed this. It felt like I was in my twenties again (that was in fact the last time I had been to a nightclub!). I have always kept up with modern music; having a 12 year old daughter probably helps although she was more into The Spice Girls and SClub7 than funky nightclub music at the time! Despite my becoming a 'dirty stop out', I was still there for my children, if occasionally a little the worse for wear! But by now, there was a big rift developing between my husband and me.

It was our 10th anniversary in August of that year although we had actually been together for seventeen years. I did from time to time through our relationship, wonder why we hadn't married sooner. Mark had asked me quite early on. I concluded that maybe I wasn't ready but now I think it more likely that I wasn't sure. We had almost split up a couple of times before, but Mark would not let me go. It was always him who convinced me that we should stay together. In fact, when I did agree to marry him, I perhaps thought that my biological clock was ticking and I wanted to have children while we were still relatively young. Having said all that, I did still love him as a person and I bought him a lovely anniversary card with words to express this. We went for a meal with the kids to celebrate. Four weeks later, however, we were apart.

You see, Jenny and I had arranged a girly weekend at her caravan in Selsey. We had had many a lovely holiday or break there, always with the kids but minus the husbands. This time however it was just Jen and me. During the day we did our usual thing of sitting in the sun, or the van, drinking wine and nattering. In the evening, we got glammed up and headed for The Embassy Club, which is where they have live entertainment and dancing at the weekends and during holiday season. It was a good night. Jen and I had a few drinks and danced the night away, as usual. It was getting towards the end of the night when Jen and I got up to dance for the last time, upon our return there were a couple of drinks waiting for us. We didn't have a clue where they had come from so we asked the girls next to us. They pointed to two relatively young men sitting a couple of tables away. They had been watching us trying to fathom out who had bought us the drinks, and were grinning like Cheshire cats!

We decided to go over and thank them, and ended up chatting to them for the rest of the night. They seemed like nice guys and I remember saying to one of them that I was old enough to be his mother! (not quite but there was an obvious age gap). He was called Dan, was pleasant looking, with a great physique and we got on really well. In fact afterwards, Jen said she had never seen two people gel so quickly in her life. So much so that I gave him my mobile number, which I had never done with anyone else I had met. I really didn't think he would call anyway so it seemed harmless enough at the time. But I was wrong... he did. In fact he called shortly after we had met to check I had given him the right number, bless! I must've made quite an impression! He lived in Berkshire, which was approximately 90 miles away so it was not going to be easy to get together but we arranged to do so anyway. Again we were going to meet in Selsey in a couple of week's time.

Meanwhile, we were regularly texting each other and I have to say that I was really looking forward to seeing him again. This time minus the Bacardi Breezer goggles! Mark, by now was very suspicious and rightly so, on this occasion his suspicions were justified. The day arrived and I arranged for Kirstie to collect the children from school and child-mind until I returned. It was a lunchtime meeting so I didn't expect to be very late back. (However, we were so reluctant to leave each other that the meeting did go on for longer than anticipated). When he first pulled up in his transit van, I suddenly felt a little nervous – I hadn't done anything like this for years! We strolled along the seafront hand in hand and then went to a quaint little pub for lunch – mostly a liquid one! He appeared a little awkward and unsure of himself so I tried to make him feel at ease. It was a glorious afternoon in every respect, but he had a long drive home and I had to get back for the children. So we said our farewells and he said he'd be in touch soon.

I arrived home to find Kirstie, or rather her children, entertaining my children. I was filling her in on all the details, when I heard the key in the lock of the front door. Mark was home. Immediately he knew something was going on as I very rarely went out socialising during the day unless it was with Kirstie, and he had phoned earlier when I had been out. Kirstie had been put on the spot and Mark had sussed that all was not as it should be. Immediately he came into the lounge demanding to know what was going on. I had consumed a couple more glasses of wine by now and was oblivious to the seriousness of the situation. He asked Kirstie to leave but for some reason I really wanted her to stay. I think it was because she was my ally in all of this. I now realise that my loyalties were misplaced. Mark was fuming. I am one of these people who really cannot have an affair - two at a time just doesn't seem right to me. Also, I am a very frank and honest individual (believe it or not!) so I asked him to leave.

After much slamming of doors and harsh words, he packed a bag and left, breaking the glass in the top of the front door as he did so. Matters had been made worse by the fact that Kirstie was one of the crowd he considered to be a bad influence. Not only that but she loved a bit of drama and I think she found the whole situation rather amusing, which in turn and with a few glasses of wine inside me, appeared to be rubbing off on me. There were also the children of course. They really had no idea what was going on and were obviously disturbed by the events of that evening. Particularly as Mark and I rarely argued, especially when they were present. It was one of the most important times when Mark and I should have been left alone to discuss our differences, and yet I chose for him to go and Kirstie to stay. What did this say about me and our relationship, I ask myself? What sort of a person had I become? And how could I treat my partner of 17 years like this?

To be honest, I have never been a very confident adult and I think I had been befriended by Kirstie and co. at a vulnerable time. They had chosen me, rather than the other way round. Although having said that, she was a good friend to me in many ways, helping with the children during my illness and being there when I needed a shoulder; plus the fact that we had common interests, we both liked to dance and sing - we had many a karaoke evening together. She had a good heart and in her own way was entertaining, maybe because she was a non-conformist like me. But she was just a little too wayward and was dragging me down the same path. I can see that now. Being 13 years her senior, I should've known better, but I have always been immature for my years and I thought perhaps that I could escape into her world for a while. She was a single mum, living in a Housing Association property but she was free, not entirely happy but free; whereas I felt like a caged bird. On the exterior her lifestyle appeared to be fun although I later discovered that she envied my life much more than I did hers.

So Mark was gone and I was left to cope with the children and the house alone. At first it seemed like a novelty, and Mark was quite accommodating with regard to the children and finances. He also allowed me the space to consider my decisions and the consequences of my actions. He was desperate for me to reconsider however, and appeared desolate at times. I was so confused and didn't want to make the wrong decision but was not ready yet to rekindle our relationship; not while I had strong feelings for someone else. Mark wrote me some beautiful letters and poetry at that time, which I still have. I didn't know he could express himself so eloquently until then. It was heartbreaking to see him so distraught. He had always been such a family man and as he himself had written 'I never wanted to be a part-time father Tina. I hate it, I absolutely hate it'. We agreed to give the separation six months and then see how we both felt. He initially stayed at his parents but after a while moved on to his sister's.

Strangely enough, I didn't feel guilt at this stage, maybe because I wasn't being deceitful – it was all out in the open. But I did feel sadness. Sadness for Mark, for the children and for all the other people this would affect. As Mark had said 'I have lost everything I care about and I don't deserve it, I have done nothing wrong.' Absolutely right, but maybe that was the problem. I, on the other hand, had done plenty wrong. I was never good at making decisions and now I had made one of the biggest and most important decisions that anyone can make: to break up our family. Did I have good enough reasons for doing this? Doubtful, yet I was resolute that I was doing the right thing. Was I just totally selfish, or was I panicking because I was not sure if or when the illness would return, and wanted to experience everything before it was too late? I still don't know the answer to these questions but I suspect the latter was probably the case.

I continued to see Dan on a regular basis. Mark had the children every other weekend, which gave me the opportunity; and once we had established that we were an item, Dan started to come down in the week as well. I also went to stay with him at his flat in Berkshire from time to time. Gradually he was introduced to my children, who took to him straight away. He was the sort of guy that I would describe as a 'cheeky chappy', if you know what I mean, always joking around and cheerful. We were not on the same wave length intellectually but did this really matter?

He made me feel good and really made me laugh. He was also very accepting of my situation, as others may not have been; in fact he told me that when I first disclosed the details of my illness to him, he just admired me and thought 'god, what has this poor woman been through'.

Dan eventually moved fairly close by as the travelling was getting ridiculous and the lease was nearly up on his rented flat in Berkshire. He rented a two-bedroom house as he also had children (three actually, he had started very young!) and wanted to have them to stay on a regular basis. Unfortunately he had had a rather acrimonious split with his wife and she was making this very difficult. However, she did occasionally relent and we got all the kids together and had some great times. Dan and I used to go out regularly to the local pub, to the Indian, or out clubbing with Kirstie and the friend that I originally met him with (who, it transpired, had bought those first drinks with the intention of snaring me for himself! I was really glad that I had chosen Dan though, even if his friend was a millionaire as I didn't like the way he operated!). There was a chemistry between Dan and I that I had never experienced with anyone before; we had just 'clicked' from day one.

However, when Mark came to mind the kids while I was off for the weekend, I did start to feel guilty about the situation. I was all dressed up in my new style of clothes, ready to meet my new man and it must've looked like I was flaunting it, which as Mark later pointed out was cruel. He was trying so hard… because he knew that Dan made me laugh, he used to tell me amusing stories in an attempt to do the same. Unfortunately, we do not share the same sense of humour. Mark, by this time, had realised that there was probably no chance of a reconciliation between us and had begun to make a new life for himself. He had met up with an old flame of his on Friends Reunited and was now renting a flat owned by one of her brothers.

This meant that finances were tight and he had, from time to time, to halve my allowance. Work was not particularly forthcoming for Dan, who was a decorator so I decided to return to work. I worked as a temp for a local agency, which meant finding a child-minder for the children. I barely earned enough to cover all the outgoings and was consequently struggling financially but there appeared to be no alternative. I knew that we could not afford to stay in the marital home and actually, this would not have felt right on a long term basis, even though Dan had now moved in as he had been finding it increasingly difficult to pay the rent on his house. I was becoming more and more stressed, trying to cope with the kids, the house and the finances and was constantly tired. I was also starting to feel low and was very short-tempered with the kids. To the point where I was losing it on occasions, which I felt very guilty about – they really didn't deserve this. We had to find a solution.

Dan's parents lived in Spain and we had been out there with the children that summer. It was a lovely part of Spain and we had all really enjoyed it. Dan had been talking to various friends about the prospect of work over there… and so the seed was planted. He knew that I was keen but that I wouldn't do it without the children, and we therefore had to convince Mark. This was not going to be easy. We did some homework into properties and schooling, and I felt confident enough to approach Mark about the subject.

But even though his new partner's family owned property over there themselves, he was not prepared to even entertain the idea. I was now in a dilemma. I could not afford to stay where I was, particularly on my own, I did not want to give up Dan but I certainly could not give up my children. However, I knew that I was going downhill fast and really not coping… I desperately needed a break and so did the children… from me.

It was therefore decided that the children would go and live with Mark and his new partner in her house, I assumed on a temporary basis, to enable me to recharge my batteries and sort my life out. I was going to join Dan in Spain. So I was standing for my dream after all but had I let my heart control my head? Undoubtedly in some ways, but I am a great believer in fate, and this I felt, had played a part. To leave my children in someone else's care was the hardest thing I have ever done and some may question how I could possibly do this. It could be considered a totally selfish act but it is very easy to judge; and unless you are in that situation, you can not even begin to contemplate what you yourself would do in similar circumstances. I am not trying to justify my decision but there are some occasions in life when you have to weigh up what is the most advantageous solution for everyone involved. This was one of those occasions.

I explained everything to the children and they seemed resigned to, even a little excited about the prospect so this made it a little easier… for them, not me. Obviously they would miss me terribly but the thought of coming out to Spain regularly to visit and having older children to annoy at home, soon put that on the backburner! I was in no fit state to be caring for them myself at this point anyway so there really was no other solution. Many parents have to work and leave their children with childminders, or work abroad and have nannies, some even send them away to boarding school; not something that I would ever have considered for my own children, but circumstances sometimes have to dictate the path your life takes and everyone, at the end of the day, has the right to choose.

Prior to this being put into action though, there was a lot of sorting out to do. The house was on the market and I was frantically trying to sell off everything that would not be needed, after Mark and the children had claimed the items that they wanted for themselves. This meant numerous car boot sales in the summer, a house clearance sale, trips to the tip as well as adverts in the paper to sell the bigger items. As you can imagine, it was a chaotic and exhausting few weeks. Mark came over at the end to remove any final items still remaining. This was both a very sad and traumatic time for me. The house was so bare, just a hollow shell of memories with no life left in it. It was also so final. And what made it worse was that Mark showed no emotion at all. He was very cold and almost detached about it. To the extent that, when his van would not start due to a flat battery and he returned to find me in floods of tears, he did not even comment. It was truly over.

Chapter 5

The Return

SO I had given in to temptation on two counts. I was not proud of myself, in fact I began to doubt my decisions as soon as I arrived in Spain and although the sun was shining and it was a lovely place to be, I could not stop thinking about Mark and the children. So much so, that I spent a great deal of time devising and writing a letter to him on the beach, while Dan was at work. It had been a long time coming. I really felt I needed to explain my actions as I had never replied to Mark's letters, and now that things were clearer in my head, I needed to voice my thoughts. There had been many sad moments during our split and I wanted Mark to know that I shared his pain.

One very poignant time was Mark's 40th birthday. He was having a party, organised by his parents and obviously I was not invited! I did text him to wish him a happy birthday and bought him a voucher for flying lessons (something he had always wanted to do) from me and the kids, and a George Michael CD from just me. 'Careless Whisper' was our song. I wanted him to know that I wasn't ready to completely let go, that I still had feelings for him – they don't disappear overnight. But all the CD succeeded in doing was upsetting him and he couldn't believe I did not want to speak to him on such an important occasion. I really felt that this would have been inappropriate as he was surrounded by family and friends, and the last thing he needed reminding of was that I wasn't there. Things were still quite raw at this stage. Then there was the first Christmas when he had dropped the children over with his dad. He had already written that he wished we were spending Christmas together and he looked so sad that I ended up in tears too.

When he had first told me that he was getting back together with his former girlfriend, I was gutted. Not because he had found another relationship, that was what I expected him to do. But the fact that it was her did not sit easy with me. They had been together for five years prior to when we met and I felt that this made a mockery of the 17 years that we had been together, and our marriage. 'Why didn't you just marry her in the first place?' I screamed 'Then we would never have met and none of this would ever have happened!' although we wouldn't have had our beautiful children either of course. The fact was that I could not believe that he would want to engage in such a committed relationship so soon, especially when he had told me that he 'loved me, more than any man could ever love me' and that I was 'the closest person he had ever had in his life'. Still, I suppose he needed to move on and I had to let him, with whomever he chose to do so.

I think I knew at this stage that his relationship would work and I was not entirely sure that mine would. In fact, if I'm honest, I resented her. She had my husband, and now my children too. I know that I was the one who instigated it all but I sincerely believe that my judgement was clouded by the illness and the fact that I was also on Prozac at the time. The last thing I wanted to do was give up my children but I knew that I not only couldn't cope with them but I also at present had nothing to offer them but my unconditional love and this was not enough; Mark on the other hand, could give them this, as well as the security and stability that they needed. I said all this in the letter although at that time, I could not bring myself to send it. The original plan had been that I would see the children every time I came back to England, which was regularly because of my hospital visits, and that they would come out to stay in the holidays, whether Mark brought them out when staying at her family's properties, I collected them, or they had accompanied flights.

So back in Spain, I was trying to make some sort of life for myself. We were initially staying at Dan's parent's house and had the top floor to ourselves. I started to help a friend of theirs out in a bar, which kept me occupied to a certain extent and Dan and I were putting flyers out to advertise his business. The evenings were spent at the local restaurants and bars and Dan and I were getting along fine, until one particular evening. Dan had quite a short fuse and I knew he could be aggressive as I had witnessed it before but never directed at me. He was also quite jealous and incredibly strong. To the extent that if someone was looking at me lecherously he would say something, or physically remove them! I like a strong man and someone who can look after himself, I actually think it's a necessity in today's world but although I appreciated being protected, this was taking things a bit far!

We also had a huge alcohol-fuelled row one night and

to prevent me leaving the house, he physically threw me up the stairs. Usually I could hold my ground ('tough bird' as he called me) but this time I was a little wary of him. I did finally manage to leave the house and headed for his parent's bar. Dan had not wanted me to leave as he knew it was dangerous for me to be wandering the streets alone in the early hours of the morning. He was right. No sooner had I got to the main road leading to the bar, when I heard a scooter approaching. Everywhere was still and silent apart from the 'pop, pop' sound of the scooter. It went past me but then stopped. The driver reversed up and started talking to me in Spanish, which I unfortunately didn't understand. I was starting to feel nervous. He then spoke in English and was offering me money. When I refused, he drove away, only to return moments later. My heart was beating faster and faster as I looked around for somewhere to hide, hearing the 'pop pop' getting louder and louder.

I knew that I could be in very real danger and was now very scared. I made up some story about having to get back to my children, one of whom was unwell, in an attempt to appeal to his sensitive side. He continued to follow me for a few more metres and then I got my phone out to call Dan. By now I feared for my safety. There was absolutely no one around, it was dark and you could've heard a pin drop. Fortunately, I think the production of the phone did the trick, after all I could've been calling anyone… the police, 'The Mob', anyone! He drove away and I have never felt so relieved in my life. Even during this ordeal, my illness crossed my mind. 'What if he tried to rip my clothes off?' I thought to myself. I had visions of me being horrified at the revulsion on his face as he discovered the secret of my mutilated body. I hurried on to the bar as quickly as I could. I did not want to return to Dan, he needed to calm down and I desperately needed a drink! Also, I was really not in the mood for an 'I told you so'!

A few days later, we were driving home when I spotted the man who had accosted me. I told Dan, who immediately braked and flew out of the car. He approached and questioned him, pointing to me cowardly sitting in the passenger seat. He denied all knowledge of the incident although it was definitely him, and Dan asked me if I wanted him to 'sort him out'. I didn't think this would be a wise move as the guy was obviously at work and his work mates could have come out to support him. Dan, on the other hand, only had me! We left it, but I think the rage on Dan's face and the size of his biceps would've made the other guy think twice about doing it again! I admired Dan's bravery but did question his sanity! This was in stark contrast to Mark who was a mild-mannered man and did not like confrontation. In fact, it was me who usually sorted out any battles as I was the more fiery of the two of us.

Back at the house, we discussed the events of the evening with his parents. I was not impressed by Dan's treatment of me and his parents did not condone it. However, in the circumstances it had probably been right to restrain me and prevent me from leaving, although the whole situation had left a distinctly sour taste in my mouth. Other things came to light that also caused me to doubt his integrity. He had told a few little white lies to keep me sweet and I didn't know how much I could trust him any more. It transpired that his wife had been out to Spain with the children and stayed at his parent's house, which he had assured me would not be happening. Of course I had no objection to the children staying there but I did not feel it was appropriate for his ex-wife to be staying under the same roof while we were having a relationship. Fortunately, I was due to come back to England for a hospital visit so it gave me the opportunity to dwell on it. But unfortunately, I had fortuitously discovered some new lumps in my neck that would require investigation.

So I flew home for the hospital appointment. Back in England, I prepared myself for the worst. I mean I'd already had cancer so what else were the lumps likely to be? Again a biopsy was performed and it was confirmed, the cancer had returned. Since the house was due to be sold and I had nowhere else to go, I went to stay with my parents in Surrey and was therefore referred to The Royal Marsden Hospital for treatment; so at least I was in good hands, I thought to myself. They started me on a new course of drugs called Letrozole. These appeared to have few side effects but I was not feeling particularly great, and decided to stay at home over the Christmas period to see if there were any cumulative effects, and to be monitored. It felt very strange not to have my own house and to be back living with my parents at 40 years of age but at least I was not alone and there was somewhere to accommodate my children.

Dan and I kept constantly in touch. He was obviously staying in Spain, where both his home and his job were. My whole family spent Christmas with my sister, Kim, which was great but I was missing Dan and it would have been nice if we could have spent the Christmas period together; but flights at that time of year are very expensive and as I was planning to return to Spain as soon as possible, it seemed a bit of a waste of money to get together for a few days when funds were so low. But I couldn't wait to get back to Spain. The way I saw it, I had been fortunate enough to have had a good 2 years of remission and maybe the Spanish lifestyle would be more conducive to recovery than grey, miserable England! Plus the fact that I was only taking tablets so I did not have to attend the hospital for treatment, which meant that I was not so restricted. The plan this time, was that Dan would find somewhere for us to live while I was in the UK (as I felt it was time we were living independently of his parents) and I would tie up any loose ends here, including getting the relevant papers for my cat to travel, and sorting out the boxes I would need in Spain. Then he would come and collect me, load up the car and we would drive back to Spain together.

I arranged the ferry crossing, which unfortunately did not go as far as Spain at that time of year so we had to travel to St. Malo and drive through France in its entirety, cross the border near Toulouse and continue on to the Costa Blanca. We were in for a long journey! When Dan arrived in England, I was so pleased to see him; it had been a lonely time without him. Especially since my children had now settled into their new lives. This, I found very difficult. They were living in a totally different area to where we had previously resided, and as a mother, it felt very unnatural to be unfamiliar with their new schools, circle of friends etc. I was sincerely hoping that I could get well enough to have the children to live back with me at some stage but they had had enough disruption in their lives thus far, and they needed a period of stability. Plus, I didn't know which way my health would go; my life was just too unpredictable.

So on February 3rd (I remember the date clearly as it was actually Mark's birthday and at the time, I thought there was something very significant about that) we headed back to Spain. Dan did all the driving as I wasn't feeling confident enough to tackle the Spanish roads – even though it was my car! I have to say that as we approached Denia, it really felt like I was coming home. The familiar sight of the Mongo (a small inhabited mountain) and the beach, filled me with excitement. This, I thought to myself, was my chance at a new life. The apartment Dan had secured for us (although he had had to sell his scooter in order to do so!) was just perfect: two bedrooms as I had requested so that the children were able to stay on a regular basis, a nice sized living area and a view from our balcony of the communal pool surrounded by palm trees – a typical Mediterranean scene. We settled in quickly, buying everything we needed (although it was part-furnished so we didn't require much but we just wanted to make it our own).

Dan continued to work but I had decided to take it easy for a while; I wasn't feeling too great. I spent my days sunbathing on the balcony (yes, it was already warm enough – well, at least in sheltered spots), reading books and resuming my role as 'the little housewife'! The evenings were again spent socialising in the local bars and catching up with new acquaintances. Dan and I were getting along fine. I think we had both had time to consider where we wanted the relationship to go, and we had ultimately decided that we just wanted to be together so we were determined to try and make it work. It was bliss, but it was sadly to be short-lived. Five weeks later the dream was over.

Chapter 6

Snakes & Ladders

YOU see, I had to come back to England for what I thought would be a routine check and to have a scan to ensure that the tablets were working. They weren't. The cancer had now spread to my liver and bones (there was a small deposit on my left scapula and sternum). This explained why I had been feeling and looking unwell in Spain and was totally lacking in energy. The lifestyle we had been leading probably exacerbated the situation as there seemed little else to do in the evenings except go from one bar or restaurant to another! I wasn't drinking excessively, but I was drinking regularly. This was obviously a critical time and a new course of life-saving treatment would be required, as once cancer has a hold on one of your major organs, you have a big battle on your hands. It now finally dawned on me that I had secondary cancer and that I was highly unlikely ever to be cured, if indeed I survived this. When it had just been a couple of lumps in my neck I could cope, but now this was serious stuff. The liver is the combustion engine of your body – if it isn't functioning properly, neither can you.

I was scared now, probably for the first time; scared

for my life, for my children, for my family and for my future (if I had one). This was a huge hurdle that I may not be able to jump over. But I was determined to fight. I wasn't ready to give up just yet. Where there's life, there's hope. I had to do it for the children. So I embarked on a new course of chemo, combined with Pamidronate for my bones and a revolutionary new drug called 'Herceptin'. This attaches to a protein on your cancer cells, preventing them from multiplying in the usual way. The chemo was Paclitaxel, or Taxol to give it its commercial name. I was going to lose all of my hair this time; the cold cap would not work with this particular type of chemo. I was also going to experience, amongst other things, flu-like symptoms and tingling in the hands and feet. Although I knew all this, I don't think I was really prepared for the onslaught I was about to endure. It was the worst experience of my life so far.

My hair started to fall out after the second treatment, again in handfuls. It was soul-destroying. I ended up looking like Gollum out of Lord of the Rings! That is the look that you always associate with cancer patients, isn't it? My sister had to come round and cut off the remaining strands which I know she found very difficult. I also discovered a birth mark on the back of my head that I never knew existed, until then! This time, I did go down the wig route but what a mistake that was! My parents and sister came with me to choose it. I then took it to a salon associated with the Marsden, to have it cut into a more trendy style. However, it felt so uncomfortable and unnatural that I was reluctant to wear it. On one occasion, I did try – Kim (my sister) and I went into Guildford but I felt ridiculous and so self-conscious that I wanted to hide. I couldn't get home fast enough. I vowed never to wear it again – and I never did.

So it was back to scarves, or bandanas as I now preferred to refer to them. But this time I had no hair to poke out of the sides and my eyebrows and eyelashes were falling out too. This leaves your face looking so bland that you can hardly recognise yourself as these are your defining features. Combined with the steroids, which completely bloat your body and face, causing your mouth to pucker and almost disappear, the result is devastating... I looked like a puffer fish! My limbs also felt very heavy due to the fluid retention.

The treatment was three-weekly and for a few days of each cycle, I hardly ventured out of bed as I felt so awful. However, on my better days I did try to make an effort; I would do a keep fit video, or go for long walks to try and keep myself as fit as possible, but also to prevent myself from going completely insane! I was literally climbing the walls. When I did go out, it was always the same route I chose; where I would not come across many other people. There was also a church en route where I would stop and say a little prayer in the doorway – always the same one 'God, if you're there, please help me get through this'. I just wanted the ground to open up and swallow me, and only regurgitate me when it was all over! I did not want to socialise and I withdrew from society as much as possible. This included Dan.

Even though he continued to phone and tried to support me, I couldn't believe that if he saw me, he would want the relationship to continue. With my looks had gone my confidence and self-esteem too. I couldn't stand the sight of myself, so he sure as hell wasn't going to find me attractive. He did offer to come over and see me but I consistently pushed him away. Our relationship had been based very much on the fact that we were physically attracted to each other; obviously it had grown into more than that as we were together for 2½ years but the treatment is so ageing – not only was I completely bald but my skin was like crepe paper and had a grey tinge to it, and being that he was so much younger than me, I couldn't bear the thought of him seeing me like this; particularly as he had always thought of me as fit and strong. I suppose that I didn't want to expose any weaknesses, or chinks in my armour, even though these were imposed by an external force, and were no fault of my own.

I know it should be about who you are and not what you look like but I felt my personality had changed as well as my appearance. I was depressed, lacking in confidence and despised myself. I almost felt like some kind of alien. This was encouraged by the reaction I received when I was out in public. People just can't help themselves, can they? Teenagers snigger, children – and unbelievably some adults – stare, which I know is only human nature but it really brought home to me what disabled people (or in fact, any person whose appearance is different from the 'norm') have to endure every single day of their lives. They can't escape; they can hide if they want to but if they did, they wouldn't be living, just existing. On the other side of the coin, as some have been like it perhaps all of their lives, they may have, over time, adapted and adjusted to it, whereas when the change is only temporary, you have something to compare it with and it is maybe not so easy to accept.

Happy Family (Before Cancer)

Kids' Birthdays (A year before the Onslaught)

South of France - The Headscarf Era
(After First Treatments)

Rhodes Town ('Unpeeled Prawns Lunch') with Jen

Faliraki - The Quiet Night

Faliraki - Girls Behaving Badly!

Karaoking to 'Immortality'

Caribbean - (Feeling conspicuous
in my Specialised Swimsuit)

Caribbean - Cheers!

My Wonderful Family – (Back Row: Kim, Me, Mark, Hannah (Hannie), Gary, Caroline, Alastair, Les, Mum & Dad. Front Row: Chris, Beth, Lauren (Loz), Christian, Dan & Kirsti (Koo)

Having Fun in Kim's Garden

In Spain with Dan

Mediterranean Woman!

Euro Disney (After liver cancer) – Sensible!

Euro Disney - Not so Sensible!

Stratford, in the Park (After brain tumour) - Me & My Boy

Stratford, in the Park - Me & My Girls

Stratford - Gary's Garden

Xmas at Kim's - With My Dad

Xmas at Kim's - With My Sister-in-Law, Caroline

The Photo Shoot - Funky!

The Photo Shoot - Wistful

The Photo Shoot – Glam!

The Photo Shoot - Glam 2!

The Photo Shoot - Sisters

I have often thought to myself, if one in three people suffers cancer at some stage in their life, where are they all? Unless you are visiting the Marsden, you rarely come across another lady wearing a bandana, or a wig (and I can now spot these a mile off!). The statistics for breast cancer in the UK are that one in nine women will develop the disease at some point in their life. That is a huge statistic amongst the female population. Where and why are we all hiding?

It would be far more accepted if we could all face it head on and literally come out of the closet. This is not a condition we asked for; we were unlucky enough to have had it inflicted upon us. How we choose to deal with it is a very personal and individual choice, and some deal with it better than others. But I truly believe that if we didn't attach such a taboo to cancer and its effects, it would make life a whole lot easier for those of us who are unfortunate enough to have to experience it. Admittedly, during treatment, sufferers probably feel too unwell to go out and about but afterwards, when the body is recovering and the hair is returning (which takes a long time in some cases), we should all be out making the most of our days – after all we do not know how many more we have left, none of us do. It's society's attitudes that sometimes prevent us from doing this.

I somehow managed to get through the treatment but during this time, Dan and I had split up. This was ultimately my doing. I remember a conversation I had had with his mum in Spain, when she had said that she really didn't think he would be able to cope with something of this magnitude. It occurred to me that maybe she was right although in hindsight I think that this should have been his decision to make. After all, he may have been younger than me, but he was not a child. I wanted the life that he had in Spain so much, but because of the illness this would not now be possible for me – the Herceptin was to continue on a 3 weekly basis and it was intravenous. It was also very expensive. However, there was no way that just because I could not fulfil my dream, I was going to prevent him from fulfilling his. So I pushed him away, as I had done with everyone else, bar my parents and my sister, who were constantly there for me. In a way, I felt as if I was setting him free – I have to live with this awful illness but he doesn't, he has a choice. I now felt totally alone.

I was one of the lucky ones though, the treatment amazingly had worked (I had a complete radiological response to therapy, which meant that there was no longer any cancer visible) and we were all obviously delighted; but now I had to try and pick up the threads of my life, and this was no easy prospect. I had slithered to the bottom of the snake and now I had one almighty ladder to climb. I was homeless, childless, jobless and manless! It was going to take a great deal of effort and an iron will to even manage to get on the first rung but I knew I had to try. My sister and family had very kindly offered for me to stay with them for a while as although I love my parents very much and they had looked after me admirably during the treatment, I needed a change and to be mixing with people of my own generation. So I moved in in August of that year. I had some recovering to do but I did not want to be a burden on what was already a very busy household so I kept pretty much to myself initially.

Having watched me go through so much suffering again,

my family including my brother, sister-in-law and nephews wanted to give me something positive to look forward to so they booked and paid for a trip for us all to go to Euro Disney. I managed to keep this a secret from my children until the very last minute – in fact until we were just about to board the Eurostar! Lauren was not impressed that I had kept it from her as she thought it made her appear babyish amongst all her grown-up cousins. But I knew that if she had been informed beforehand, she wouldn't have given anyone a moment's peace!

It is such a magical place that it even exceeded the Caribbean in Lauren's estimation (she loves theme parks). We had a brilliant, if exhausting few days, certainly a time to remember and it made me realise just what a special family I had. I had always known this but it really brought it home to me. My brother, Gary, and his family had also been very supportive during this last phase of the illness. Even though they live in Stratford-Upon-Avon, they would find time to come down and visit. Gary even came down on his own from time to time, and just sat in the garden with me. They also bought me a very thoughtful present of a portable radio/CD player, which he tuned in to certain programmes intended to cheer me up.

So I was attempting to get on with some sort of a life and Jenny had offered me the use of her caravan anytime in the summer holidays. I had already spent a few days there with her and her children earlier in the summer, which had worried her as I was feeling very low and agitated, almost certainly due to the medication I was taking. However, I decided to take her up on her offer as I felt this might be a good place to recuperate. So I went down to Selsey alone. Big mistake! The weather was not great and I felt trapped in the confines of the caravan.

Not only that but it just evoked too many memories that at that time I was struggling to cope with. I did go into the village and visited East Beach, where Dan and I had met on our first date but without the children's laughter and Jen's company, it all seemed very flat. I went to the Ocean Bar in the evening and got chatting to a couple of people, who although I was still wearing a bandana, did not realise that I had been ill. This was a little light relief but I knew that I didn't want to be there so I texted Kim. She and Les, her husband, drove down the very next morning to collect me. I should perhaps have known that I wasn't quite ready for that. One step at a time, as my sister kept saying.

Throughout the summer, such as it was, I was slowly recovering and getting my stamina back. My mental state was still a little suspect though! As I have mentioned earlier, I have such an active mind that I have to be doing something, otherwise I feel like I'm wasting time so I decided that once the summer holidays were over, I would attempt to get a job. Easier said than done in my situation but this I did; in fact I got two – obviously both part-time – but one was to be short-lived. Although I had been very honest about my condition and was still wearing a bandana at the interview, the illness again got in the way. My regular visits to the hospital just interfered too much with my hours, especially since the clinics do not often run to time, plus the fact that there was a slight clash of personalities and we mutually decided that it wasn't working. The other job, however, turned out to be a blessing in disguise.

I was working as a carer for a disabled lady called Sharon who had a condition called Arthrogrytosis and was wheelchair bound. Her partner had Huntington's Chorea but was still fairly mobile at this stage. At first, it was just a couple of evenings a week, helping to prepare their evening meal, feeding Sharon, assisting with her mail and her personal hygiene etc. But as we got to know each other better and my health was improving, the hours and the duties increased. I attended her place of work, gave her facials (using my old skills as a beauty therapist) and began to drive their disabled vehicle so that I was able to accompany them to appointments and on excursions. This culminated in my driving them and two other disabled people down to Devon for a 10 day break. Sharon and I got on very well and I totally enjoyed my time with her. She had such a positive outlook on life and the experience opened up a whole new world for me, which was just what I needed at that time. She had become not just my employer, but my friend.

During the October half-term, I decided to give the kids another treat. We had never actually been abroad with Jen and her children so we decided to book a holiday for us all. Sharon had very kindly allowed me the time off for this even though I had not been working for her for very long. We went to Kos, another surprise for Lauren that she was not too happy about – it was a conspiracy! Our children are all very close as they have known each other all their lives and there is little age gap between the two girls (or should I say young ladies?) and the boys. It was another all-inclusive, which was great as it gave them some independence; the boys would wander off on the complex and come back armed with hotdogs and chips etc! They thought it was fantastic. We met a group of youngsters who befriended our children, especially the girls, and us. They were a smashing group and thought we were 'well cool mums!' We would socialise with them in the evenings particularly, and when we had to move hotels half way through the holiday (how inconvenient!), they moved with us. I also somehow managed to find myself another admirer, or two, but I really wasn't interested.

Back home I continued to work for Sharon but unfortunately this job was not to last either. Upon our return from the Devon trip which was in the following March, I started to develop headaches and was having a few problems with my co-ordination and vision; to the point where I was actually dropping and bumping into things. The headaches became so severe that it was painful to even lift my head up off the pillow. My sister, obviously very concerned, decided to take me to the local hospital to be checked out. They concluded that because I was not actually vomiting, it was unlikely to be related to my cancer so they sent me off packing with some painkillers although they did suggest that if the headaches persisted, I should contact the Marsden. They did, so of course I did contact the Marsden and they called me in almost immediately. So there was another snake hissing at my door and although I had managed to climb to the second rung of the ladder, I was about to slide right back down to square one.

PART THREE

'Fulfil your destiny,
Is there within the child,
My storm will never end,
My fate is on the wind…'

Chapter 7

Lost

THROUGH all of this, I was really struggling to come to terms with the effects of what I had done to the people closest to me. I am actually a very family orientated person (surprising though that may seem) and I couldn't now believe that I had split my own family up, and caused so many people so much distress. My son, when asked how it felt to be living apart from me, once said 'it feels like I'm lost in the jungle' and now I could really relate to that. I was living in someone else's house, with someone else's family – having Sunday lunch with them, when I should have been having it with my own. Although my children came to stay every other weekend, when we were apart there was a huge void in my life that nothing else could fill. I suspect there was also a void in theirs too. Having said that, they were living in a family unit, Mark's partner had two teenage children with whom they appeared to get on well, they liked their new schools and seemed to have adjusted very well to their new lives.

I, on the other hand, had not. The realisation that my children may be living apart from me on a permanent basis was heartbreaking. When you have secondary cancer, it is not only the actual illness that makes life difficult. There are also practical implications. When Mark and I sold the house, we split the equity 50/50 even though he had the children, as the prospect of me gaining regular employment was unlikely. Not only that, but I was unable to obtain a 'normal' mortgage. The amount of equity I came out with was nowhere near enough to secure me alternative accommodation, yet I was unable to claim benefits because I had this. It's a catch 22 situation. Many of my belongings were also still in Spain, including my car and my cat. In fact I never did get it all back; the car was torched in Spain, and I didn't feel it was fair to put my cat through 6 months quarantine at his age as he is approximately 20 years old (I had originally only got him a one-way ticket as I wasn't intending to return so soon) so he was re-homed and the car was replaced.

There is also the unpredictability of the illness to consider. There had been times when I was physically unable to care for my children, and there were likely to be more of these times in the future. Furthermore, even if I became well again, my earning potential was never going to match that of my husband and his partner. He had landed very much on his feet, while I had fallen flat on my face. What goes around, comes around I suppose. Good luck to him but now I felt like I was being punished. I had already tortured myself, over and over again; churning it all over in my mind endlessly. What I had done was wrong but now it was too late; I had panicked and we all now had to live with the consequences. None of us knew how this would affect the children in the future.

It also left me in a very difficult predicament that I had

not even contemplated at the time of the split. The only way I could acquire a home for myself now that I was alone, was through the council or housing associations. It would also only be a one-bedroom place as the children did not reside with me permanently. This meant that it was likely to be very small and would not accommodate them very well when they stayed. I could of course, rent privately, but this is so expensive that my present funds would not last five minutes if I were to do so and then what would I use to live on, on a day to day basis? I was stuck in a hole that there seemed no way out of. Maybe this was payback time I thought to myself.

Looking at it from the other viewpoint though, what I had done could be considered a good thing. In some ways I had been very selfless. I had given the children the opportunity of a better life. They now lived in a four bedroom house, had all the luxuries of modern day living and went to very good schools so were getting a high standard of education. Mark had a partner and the family unit he had always yearned for, and the children had acquired an extended family. Not only that but like Dan, I had set them free from the illness. Mark did not have to care for me any longer, and the children did not have to watch me go through the horrendous treatment (I only saw them on the good days). I wasn't planning to disrupt their lives again; they had had enough to cope with already. I wanted them to have some consistency in a stable environment, which again, I was unable to provide. So maybe I wasn't this wicked person after all. The only person, it appeared, whose life was in tatters as a result of my actions and the illness, was me.

On the positive side, one good thing that had occurred as a result of all this was that since I had been living with my sister and family, a closeness had developed both between myself, my children and her family. Although I was in this wilderness, they had taken me and the children into the heart of their family and cocooned us in love. My sister, through no fault of her own, was unable to help very much physically the first time round as she just lived too far away, but this time she was determined to be with me every step of the way. She is a very beautiful person – inside and out, and she helped me through some very difficult times, which I know were also profoundly difficult for her. We have had some great (and also, on occasions, some very sad) times but whatever the circumstances, there is always an underlying kindness and compassion within their household that I believe is rare to find. We would go on bike rides together; the youngest daughter, Beth, would sleep over in what we had appropriately named The Den (which is the space I occupy in their house) and we would also sometimes just 'be'.

Kim and I have shared some very poignant and special moments. In fact, relationships with everyone close to you intensify; I suppose there is an urgency and a need to say all those things that you have only previously thought. My friendship with Jenny grew as did my relationship with Mark's sister Karen, who I had always considered my friend as well as my sister-in-law, even after the split. There has always been a bond between us and this was well and truly cemented when she was also diagnosed with breast cancer. We understood each other and could totally relate to all the emotions we experienced during our ordeals; the peaks, the troughs and everything in between. We would visit each other in hospital and share jokes about our condition, which only people with cancer would appreciate and would be allowed to tell! She actually invented a few new words to the Snowman song, which went something like this:

'I'm walking in the air; I haven't any hair at all;
In fact I'm totally bald, a slap head I am called!'

We would drive along singing this at the top of our voices. She always did have a great sense of humour, which I believe is helping her through her own personal battle. I was also able to express my love for my children, without getting irritable with them – the time we now had together was special time. I was able to do some things for them that I would previously not have contemplated for financial reasons. Lauren had always wanted to go horse-riding – she is a real animal lover; and Chris is very agile (a bit like Spiderman, who had been one of his heroes when he was younger!) so I booked them both a course in horse-riding and rock climbing respectively. It was actually the main part of their Christmas present and was a complete surprise to them both. They were obviously delighted and couldn't wait to start. I had decided that I was going to spend some of the money I had, on just doing pleasurable and memorable things. After all, a few hundred pounds was not going to make any difference to my situation. In order to re-house myself and to make a difference, I would need tens of thousands and this was not likely to be very forthcoming!

You see, when you have a life threatening illness, your whole perspective changes… I know it's a bit of a cliché but it's the truth. Things that were important before become insignificant and futile; your priorities change; you look at the whole world through different eyes. There is a realisation that people are the most important thing in life, and I was fortunate enough to have some very special people in mine. My sister would say that the most important thing 'is to love and be loved'. I am totally with her on that one. The little things you do in life that show how much you care for someone can really touch their heart. Kim and family did one such thing for me at Christmas time. I don't usually have a stocking as I thought these were the children's domain, but Kim's family all have one and so that I wouldn't feel left out, they got one for me too. Her two teenage girls also made me a cushion with a picture of us all at Euro Disney on one side and a beautiful poem on the other. These are the type of things that make a difference and sustain you through desperate times… and each of them has left an indelible mark on my soul.

Despite this, I couldn't help waking up every morning and feeling completely and utterly lost, in every sense of the word. I wasn't that familiar with the area I was now living in so I was, in a way, on unknown territory; I no longer had a job or a role so had no purpose or structure to my day; I had many acquaintances but few friends locally, which made socialising difficult and most of all I missed my children desperately. The fact is that I had no control over what was going to happen to me, my destiny was to be decided by a greater force. What I had done for the children, as it turned out, had been the right thing to do. They were safe and secure. Happy? Not entirely but unless Mark and I were going to get back together and the illness eradicated from my body, and this was highly unlikely to happen, their lives were never going to be perfect.

At the end of the day, I had acted in their best interests, even though I did receive some criticism along the way (but only from the ignorant). Not only that, but the children were experiencing what it was like not to be with me 24/7, which was perhaps a period of adjustment for them, in preparation for the time when I may not be around at all… God forbid. It had to be this way, there was no alternative. My whole life was about to come crashing down again but I believe in fate and this did not need to directly affect everybody else's life. The children were sheltered from it and although we had discussed it, they did not need to know the severity, or the possible consequences, of what was about to happen.

It was actually my and my sister's birthday that weekend (coincidentally, Lauren and Chris's birthdays are just two days apart and it may even have been 1 day like us if he could've got out on his own!). I had been admitted to the Marsden under observation a couple of days previously. They were controlling the headaches, and the other symptoms that I mentioned earlier, with steroids but as you had probably guessed, the scan revealed that I now had a brain tumour. Fortunately, it was operable, just lying on the surface, and my body had very cleverly formed a cyst around it so that there were no tendrils probing deeper into my brain. Even so, it was obviously devastating news. In fact, this is the first time that I had ever seen my father cry.

They were waiting for a bed to become available at the Atkinson Morley Hospital, which is where the surgery was to be performed so they allowed me out for the weekend. It was May 1st, my sister's birthday, and it was a beautiful day so Kim decided we should take a picnic to Hampton Court. This we did and it was lovely to be relaxing in the sunshine. It was quite an emotionally charged day because of the circumstances but due to the calmness of the surroundings and the almost tangible love that enveloped us, we were able to keep this in check. The importance of what I was about to undergo was evident to us all, but it remained unspoken. It had already been said.

We were just enjoying a boat ride along the Thames, with Chris cuddled up to me, when Kim received a call. It was my parents telling us that the hospital was ready for me and we should therefore make our way back as soon as possible. My parents were to take me as they wanted to be with me but also because Kim had a houseful, including my two. First though we had the present opening session as I was now going to be in hospital on my actual birthday. Just as well we did as I had been bought some very thoughtful and appropriate gifts, including a stylish weekend case, funky pj's, dressing gown and some slippers. So I packed all these and my birthday cards up and steeled myself for this next round of the fight. You see, I know that brain surgery is such an intricate and exact science that the slightest error can have severe implications. Now my fate really did lie in the hands of the surgeons and the lap of the gods.

Chapter 8

God's Waiting Room

SO I arrived at the Atkinson Morley Hospital, which was a complete contrast to the Marsden. Whereas the Marsden is an older style building, with standard type wards but exceptional staff, the Neurosurgery wing of the AMH, which is relatively new, is very white and clinical and very hi-tech – you almost need a diploma to operate the TV! People come from all over the world to have brain surgery here so I felt it was a privilege that I was receiving such high quality care. Having said that, the surgery I was due to have must have warranted it.

The first day was obviously spent just settling in although the nurses had said that I would be having a scan – which never happened. I felt it was a bit of a waste of my birthday really to be stuck in hospital with very little happening, but they obviously wanted to secure the bed for me and it was also a Bank Holiday so what did I expect? As it was a lovely day, I did take myself off for a walk. That part of Tooting however, has very little to offer it would appear and I didn't want to wander too far in case they needed to perform some tests on me, or something. So I returned to the ward and arranged all my birthday cards and flowers on the window sill (like you do!), properly unpacked my case and managed to get the hi-tech TV to work, which was a feat in itself! I also got chatting to the people in the adjacent beds, which was both interesting and enlightening.

The nurses did come round and do the usual blood pressure tests etc. and eventually I saw the doctor, who explained the procedure they were about to undertake. I asked to see the scan that apparently had been forwarded on from the Marsden (which might explain why they didn't need to do another one) as I like to know exactly what is going on, after all it is my body. And a pretty amazing one it is too, I have decided. You see, from the scan, I could clearly see the cyst that my body had formed around the tumour, apparently protecting my brain from the cancer. I have said before that my body appears to dislike being invaded by foreign objects or substances; it seems to reject them one way or another. In some instances, this can be detrimental to what is trying to be achieved but in this case, it was a blessing. The fact that the cyst was there was going to make removal of the tumour more straightforward, and for this one thing alone, I was very grateful.

You see, when you look around you in a place like that, you become very aware of the skill that is required by the highly qualified surgeons and the vast array of cases they have to deal with. During my stay alone, there were brain tumours and spinal injuries – all of a different variety and severity. The results of their very intricate work can have drastic effects on the lives of their patients, which is a tremendous responsibility for them to bear. Venturing into the brain must also be a bit of an unknown quantity; they therefore are learning all the time, but I find it incredible that they can achieve such amazing results, and save or prolong the lives of so many individuals, and in so doing, greatly improve their quality of life. My surgery was scheduled for the next morning, and although I was obviously anxious about the outcome, I had faith in the surgeon and just prayed that there would be no complications.

I was first to go down to theatre that morning so was awoken early. I had a shower and the nurses then came along to prepare me. It did cross my mind that this could possibly be the last time that I would have all my faculties intact and therefore be the 'Tina' that everybody knew and loved. A scary thought but I had been assured that the procedure was quite standard in my case so I tried to push this thought to the back of my mind. I just couldn't quite believe the speed at which it was all happening though. Things had progressed so fast from diagnosis to surgery. Perhaps this was a good thing as it didn't give me time to mull over the possible consequences. I am not renowned for my positivity but somehow at crucial times, I manage to summon some up from somewhere! I was determined to pull through this.

Herceptin had worked wonders on the cancer in the rest of my body but it does not work in the brain, due to the blood/brain barrier. This is a barrier whose function it is to protect the brain from intruders but unfortunately, it also prevents most medication from reaching and potentially destroying those intruders. This means that the usual remedy for secondary brain tumours is removal and/or radiotherapy. My tumour was in the top right-hand part of my brain, thankfully at the back of my head and to give it its medical name, a parietal metastasectomy was about to be performed. This would involve shaving my head in that region, breaking my skull and giving me a flip-top; so I knew I would awake with another very interesting hairstyle! I was quite calm as I was taken down to theatre; I had already said a prayer and prepared myself as much as anyone can. Now my fate would be decided by someone, or something greater.

When I did come round, I was amazed at how well I felt… all things considered! I was relieved that I appeared to have all my faculties and delighted when I was told that the operation had been a great success. I was sent back to the recovery ward, where the nurses can keep a close eye on you, and left to rest and recover in my own time. My parents were anxious to make sure that I was ok so they came up to see me and could not quite believe the speed at which I appeared to be recovering. I was already sitting up in bed when they arrived, and they too were relieved that all my faculties were intact. I hadn't changed at all apart from the obvious bandage, rather like a turban, on the top of my head and a space in my brain which the tumour had previously occupied. Again, I considered myself to be very lucky – others aren't always quite so fortunate.

Among the other patients, there was a young girl from the Caribbean, who had suffered a brain haemorrhage and had been in hospital for six months so far. Her head was very swollen on the right side and she had a large scar as a result of her surgery. Not only that, but she had problems with her speech and mobility, had a withered right hand and appeared to be slightly incontinent. She was only 19 years old. Another older patient had had a brain tumour removed 20 years ago but had developed another one and the removal of this had left her with dizziness, and consequently, mobility problems. Then there was the lady from Gibraltar whose vision had been seriously affected. It was touch and go for a while as to whether she would lose her sight altogether. Thankfully she did regain some vision before I left. Another relatively young lady had a tumour on her spine. This had left her practically paralysed on her left side so that she required a frame or a walking stick to assist her movement; and finally there was Betty, who like me, had had a brain tumour, the removal of which had caused her entire face to puff up and turn purple. Although mine was the only malignant tumour, I appeared to have come off better than most.

Despite this, they all continued to smile and laugh and make jokes about their predicament. Betty said she had never felt so ugly in her life! Although there were serious moments too, the atmosphere on the whole was fairly light-hearted. None of us wanted pity, just understanding and kindness. When you are a patient in hospital for any period of time, there is a camaraderie that quickly develops between yourself and the other patients, which may not occur in any other circumstances. You feel the need to assist and support each other in any way you can. This extended to making hot drinks, sharing sweets and other goodies with each other, and getting visitors to restock any supplies that were getting low! You knew that when you left the hospital, the relationships would cease, after all we had all just been thrown together by circumstances, but the memory of the friendships we had made would stay with us. I was full of admiration for them all. How courageous they all were. And how lucky was I?

Time seemed to move so slowly just lying there in my hospital bed. The nights seemed endless. Sleep would evade me and I would listen to the silence, or the hushed voices in the semi-darkness. If I did sleep, I would have the most bizarre dreams and awake with a start, wondering if it had really happened. With so much time to think, it was here that I decided I was going to write a book. It had always been an ambition of mine but only now did I feel I had enough material and the time to dedicate to it. I wanted to share my experiences with others, in the hope that it may help in some way. I also decided that if my life was going to be shortened by this illness, I wanted to leave something behind for my children, my family and my friends. I felt it would help them to understand why I had made the decisions I had and how I actually felt throughout the entire ordeal; as although you can tell them, spoken words can so easily be forgotten. If it is there in black and white, it is permanent and can be revisited time and time again.

Because I was doing so well, the doctors decided that I could go home the following day. It seemed a little early to me but I had to trust their judgement. Unfortunately however, that morning I experienced some blurred vision so they decided to keep me in under observation. Actually it was just as well they did as that night I had a seriously leaky head! I was due to go back to my parent's house but my mum would have freaked if she had been faced with a pillow full of blood. Not to mention the mess it would have made! The doctors were concerned about this as I could have been haemorrhaging. They had to keep changing the bandages as they were just completely soaked and there was talk of taking me back into theatre to put more staples in. After a time, they did manage to stem the flow and agreed that it was just a leaking artery so, much to my relief, it was concluded that no further intervention would be necessary.

I had by now, moved bed 3 times in as many days! I suppose it was a change of scenery if nothing else! My visitors had included my parents, of course, my sister and Karen, my sister-in-law. The children had not been brought in to see me as Chris was away on a PGL trip, to which my husband had also gone as a helper. It was probably just as well as it might have been a little disturbing for them… although I could've done with a hug. Mark and I had had an emotional discussion prior to my going into hospital about how we would approach this with the children, and decided that honesty was the best policy but obviously without worrying them unduly. Jen had already come to see me in the Marsden before I was transferred to the AMH and was planning to visit again once I was home.

During Karen's visit we went outside, sat on a bench, had a cigarette and chatted for a while. It did cross my mind that this must be quite difficult for her. I wondered if she was thinking that this might be where she was heading. I sincerely hope not. As ever, she was great company and we managed to have a giggle together. My sister was wonderful, bringing up clean clothing, flowers etc. One of the other patients thought we looked so much alike that we could be twins. I felt this was a bit of an insult to her at the time as I obviously was not looking my best! We are very alike although you can definitely tell who the healthy one is!

This whole episode was without a doubt the most surreal experience of my life. I couldn't quite believe that I had survived it so well. In fact I was just relieved that I had survived it at all and come through it pretty much unscathed. I did have a bit of a strange hairstyle and a large scar in the shape of a 'C' on the back of my head, much to Chris's delight! But I was still me and was no longer experiencing any symptoms. All that remained now, was to have the staples removed at my GP's and then to commence a 5 day course of radiotherapy. Having the staples removed was pretty painless although the scar was still a little tender. It's amazing how when you need to avoid an area though, you manage to continually knock it. I must've banged my head at least three times in the space of a week! Still, no damage was done; it may actually have knocked some sense into me!

So on to the course of radiotherapy. Uh oh, more hair loss. And the nurse did inform me that this could actually be permanent. I almost refused to go ahead on that basis. Temporary hair loss was bad enough, but permanent hair loss I really couldn't cope with. It was only after I had discussed it in more detail with the doctor that I was prepared to undergo the course of treatment. She assured me that I would be having a relatively low dose of radiotherapy, and that in these circumstances the hair loss was rarely permanent, although it may take a while to grow back. So here we go again I thought to myself. I was going to be a slap head for a third time!

The treatment itself was painless enough, if a little claustrophobic (they put a moulded mask over your entire face to protect it from the radiation) but the effect would be the same. All I ever wanted to do was to get on with some kind of 'normal' life but this, it seemed, was to evade me. What's more, I was due to go away for the weekend with Sharon shortly afterwards and knew that I would enjoy it a whole lot more with hair!

The thing is, when you have a brain tumour removed, you have absolutely no idea what the outcome will be. Anything, it appears, can and does, happen. It is also a well-known fact that it can and probably will, return in the future. Living with this thought, in fact living with secondary cancer full stop, is like living with a time bomb. You really do not know what is going to happen next. You can not plan too far ahead as so often your plans are scuppered. All you can do is jump over each hurdle as it arises, and hope that the treatment will work. It is all just so unpredictable and you know that unless they find a cure, which is unlikely to happen in my lifetime anyway, you will have it for life.

And yet, all the time you are learning and growing, making new relationships, evaluating your life and, in my case, wondering what can still be achieved. It seemed that there was so much still to do and perhaps not enough time to do it. But you have to think positively otherwise you might as well just curl up in a ball and give up all together. This, I am proud to say, is not in my nature although at times, it has seemed like a tempting proposition!

Chapter 9

Stripped Bare

IT IS 5.45am 20th December 2005 and I have awoken to the sound of my teenage niece partying with her friends. Sleep is now eluding me so I felt compelled to continue writing this. My children and Beth are asleep in The Den, it's dark and silent and I am surrounded by Christmas decorations and wrapped presents under the tree. I feel pensive but also apprehensive as I have decided to discontinue taking my medication until after the festivities are over, and am debating whether this is the right thing to do. The tablets make me feel unwell and I did not want anything to interfere with the enjoyment of the season. I recently had a blip where I had to spend the day in bed and obviously do not want a repeat performance while my children are here. I have got them for a week so will be spending Christmas day with them, which will be wonderful if all goes to plan.

The only problem is that I am obviously concerned that all the time I am not taking the medication the cancer may be advancing. This thought has been prompted by the fact that I have been experiencing slight headaches again. This is the constant worry of living with secondary cancer; you never know whether to attribute symptoms to the illness or not. A recent bout of sickness and diarrhoea was automatically attributed to the tablets but it turned out to be a bug – my brother-in-law experienced the same symptoms. I'm therefore hoping that this is just a normal headache, and trusting that one week's abstinence won't make much difference. All will be revealed in the fullness of time.

So back to the job in hand. After the radiotherapy, I did go away for the weekend with Sharon and co. as arranged. It was actually a weekend at Butlins in Bognor called a Hot Summer Party – literally down the road from where I used to live with my family. Various bands were playing throughout the weekend and it promised to be great fun. There was a complete party atmosphere and we all got into the swing of things very quickly! There were various groups of people celebrating, including hen parties, and many were wearing fancy dress and multi-coloured wigs etc. This was rather fortunate, as a couple of days before we arrived my hair began to fall out. (Nothing it would seem goes my way!). The first night I managed to salvage enough to have wisps protruding from my bandana but by the second night I had lost these as well! It was very disheartening but I was not going to let it spoil the weekend – with, or without hair, I was determined to enjoy myself.

One of the bands due to be playing was Heatwave, of 'Always and Forever' fame. In fact they had also played on my last holiday with Sharon and this I'm sure was one of the reasons she still invited me, even though I was no longer working for her. You see I had met two of the band members (not the original members I hasten to add!) at this previous gig. After they had performed, we went into the nightclub for a dance and they were in there. I was dancing away, oblivious to what was going on around me, when one of them approached me and we began to chat. He asked for my phone number, which I declined – for no other reason than the fact that I really did not feel I was in a position to be making new liaisons at that time. But they did not give up easily as the second band member then pursued me. He too asked for my number, and whilst this was very flattering, I was sure that if he realised that what he was seeing was not actually what he would be getting, he would not be so interested. Again I declined, much to Sharon's amazement.

Afterwards she said to me 'Did you know who they were?!' As if I should be in awe of them or something. I did know who they were but they did not know who I was. I was being revisited by that feeling of being a fraud – I looked good on the surface but was carrying a whole load of baggage underneath.

The second meeting however, did turn out a little differently. During their performance, for which we had a bird's-eye view being right in front of the stage, I had quite a lot of eye contact with the second of the two band members that I had met before, the other I think had either not recognised me, or had just not seen me. After the gig some of the band came and joined us for a chat and it was then that a glimmer of recognition crossed the second band member's face. At first he said that he hadn't realised that it was me, he just thought that he had pulled! But then he asked 'Are you going to give me your number this time?' He seemed like a nice guy and was obviously now aware of my situation (the lack of hair and the bandana might've been a bit of a giveaway!). So this time I obliged. Meanwhile, Sharon had disappeared off somewhere, and he left us to talk to other people.

Shortly afterwards Sharon returned with the first band member in tow. It transpired that she had found him by the amusements and had been talking to him about me; she was determined that I should not miss the opportunity of meeting him again. She had prepared him by telling him about the tough time I had been having, and I was surprised to learn that he not only remembered me but my name too (which is more than I had!). We got chatting and Sharon and co. decided to leave us to it. We went on to the nightclub and danced and chatted some more. He then walked me back to my chalet where we parted company.

He was aware that his co-band member had my number and therefore did not ask for it himself. I was a little uncomfortable about this. Maybe after spending some time with me he had realised that I was not who he had imagined me to be – preconceptions can sometimes be very different from reality, can't they? Or maybe there was a little bit of competition going on between them. I guess I'll never know as the first band member and I haven't been in contact since although the second has since become a friend. He assures me that there is no competition on his part (but would he admit it if there was?!). Not that I'm that good a catch!

The entire weekend was such fun and again very flattering for me. Not only did I meet the guys from Heatwave but I met a captain from the army on the first night and a really nice guy from Southampton on the last night. They, it seemed, did not realise that I was wearing a bandana for cancer reasons but just thought it was a fashion statement! As I said before, many people were wearing head gear in one form or another. However, I was very honest about my predicament, which gave them the opportunity to bow out gracefully if they could not cope with it. This turned out to be the case (or so I thought at the time.)

Although I have occasionally been in contact with the latter, this has only been via text messages. The captain was based in Scotland so this was going to be a no-go anyway. Plus the fact that he had a kilt on the second night and I'm afraid that I really can not do men in skirts (apologies to all Scots readers out there!). I felt very flat when I returned from this weekend. The illness did, I thought, seem to put people off; so was I destined to be alone for the remainder of my life? I sincerely hoped not.

Perhaps I was assuming too much. After all, there were other factors involved. I wasn't particularly interested in the army captain anyway, and he did in fact invite me back for a coffee the second night so he can't have been that put off (not that I went but it was nice to be asked), and the other guy lived too far away for it to be practical (especially with me not driving) and had been through a fairly recent marriage break up so he had issues. The second member of Heatwave kept in contact for a while and seemed quite keen so maybe I was putting obstacles where there weren't really any. Let's face it, many people have illnesses of one kind or another – particularly as we get older – and it doesn't seem to stop them having relationships. Why should I be any different?

This whole experience had left me feeling very vulnerable though. The very first time I had felt like this was when Jen and I were at the caravan with the kids and we took them swimming. I had decided to try a new stick-on prosthesis, thinking that this may make me feel more confident in the water - as with the type that you put into a pocket of the swimsuit, it can feel a little heavier than your natural breast and therefore look unbalanced. (This was before any attempt at reconstruction had been made). Unfortunately, it came unstuck whilst in the pool but luckily it didn't come out of the costume! That could've been very embarrassing. It was actually quite comical at the time as I was hanging on to it for dear life, but it also brought home to me that I was different and made me question whether a new partner would be able to accept this, if I myself was struggling with it. I just so wanted my own breast back. Like the wig, I never used this prosthesis again.

At Butlins, someone had asked me if I was in disguise. I got the nickname Mystic Meg from a group of young lads! I must admit, I did look a bit like a fortune-teller with my dark glasses, hoop earrings and bandana. The problem is that in a way they were right, I was trying to disguise myself. If I gave the impression that I was someone else, perhaps I could pretend that it wasn't happening to me. It's this hiding away tendency again. I did this during my second course of chemo when I stayed with my parents. I would wear dark glasses and only go where I thought I would encounter the minimum people. But however much you try to hide, eventually you have to face it. This was the course my life was going to take and I had to try to accept it.

I had been stripped of so many things since the illness began. The external symptoms were just the tip of the iceberg. I had lost the day-to-day physical contact with my children, and my best friend of 17 years. The turning point for me had been when I described Mark's new partner as 'a nightmare' after we had had an argument on the phone. He had replied, 'No Tine, you're the nightmare.' This felt like the final betrayal and I knew at this point exactly where his loyalties now lay. My opinion didn't seem to count for very much any longer. It was as if he and his new partner were trying to completely take over the care of my children, and I had very little input. This was not only hurtful but I felt it was insensitive, especially in my circumstances. I knew that it wasn't an easy situation for any of us but sometimes I wished they could show a little more compassion. In fact, if I could put them into my shoes for a day, perhaps they would realise just how difficult this whole situation is for me.

You see, I was again hairless, jobless, still living with my sister and not in a relationship. I had no purpose and too much time to think. Plus this time, I really didn't know if my hair would return. Not only that, but my driving licence now had to be withdrawn (anyone who undergoes brain surgery has to forfeit the right to drive). This was the final straw. Originally I had been told that providing I had no fits or convulsions, I could reapply in six months. This however turned out to be false information. I was trapped, or that was how it felt. The area in which we live is very rural, the train station is a mile and a half away and the buses are very few and far between. You do not realise the convenience of driving until you are unable to do it. I had wanted to see my children more often but this was going to put paid to that and to the prospect of working for Sharon again – she needed a driver and although I had applied for a few other jobs, there had been no response. I really did feel like I had been put on the scrapheap of life. And to top all the other things that had been taken away from me, I had now also lost my independence.

I was feeling really low and just a little sorry for myself at this point, whether this was justified I don't know but I felt I had already been through enough, without further obstacles being put in the way. A very kind friend of my sister's could see the difficulties I was experiencing and was in need of a little help herself; so knowing my experience of care work, she asked if I would be interested in looking after her 85 year old mother who had just returned home from a stay in hospital. It seemed the ideal opportunity to get back out there, so I agreed. It entailed caring for her mother's basic needs but not her personal care, and I would be required to stay overnight, which solved the transport problem (her daughter would take me to and from her home). Obviously, knowing my own health situation, they did not want me to overdo it, just to be there for her and do the essentials. I therefore was taken to meet her and we got along very well.

She was a delightful lady and amazing for her age but I am one of those people who have to be 'doing' so I probably did overdo it a bit. It was fairly hot on occasions so we would eat lunch in the garden when she was up to it; but then I would stay out there and do a little gardening, or take myself off for a walk into Guildford, while she rested. As time wore on though, I began to feel more depressed and less enthusiastic and I was experiencing problems with my breathing to the extent that it was starting to affect my pursuits. Despite the fact that Herceptin had cleared the cancer in my soft tissues, it can have a detrimental affect on the heart, due to its toxicity. This culminated in my nearly keeling over when I went for a bike ride with my son and my sister's family on a particularly hot summer's day. It was not only frightening for me, but very scary for my son. It was all just a little too much too soon; and it was at this point that I decided to take control of my own healthcare. I wanted to have a break from Herceptin.

I was by now really depressed. I don't know whether it was the prospect of being alone and wondering how I would cope, but the crux came when everyone was about to go on their summer holidays – everyone's holiday dates seemed to coincide so that my kids, Kim's family and Jen were all away at the same time. I did not have a family to go on holiday with and this made me feel very sad. I felt at such a loss and if ever there was a time that I wanted to give up, this was it. I felt generally unwell anyway but coupled with the depression, I was reluctant to even get out of bed. What was the point? I couldn't do anything I wanted to anymore, or so it seemed.

There was a time, before the illness, when I could've done anything with my life – the world was my oyster – but I didn't do it. Now that I wanted to, I couldn't. I had procrastinated (or 'contemplated my navel' as my husband would say) for far too long and now it was too late. I felt that the best years of my life had been wasted. I was desperate and in dire need of some t.l.c so my parents (as usual) came and rescued me and tried to nurse me back to health.

It took a while and a trip to the doctors before I began to feel a little more positive. But the true tonic was when my hair finally began to grow. I cannot tell you how relieved I was. Just the faintest shadow but it was definitely there! So I was not going to be permanently bald after all. I had a bit of what you might call an anti-Mohican for a while and a few dents in my head but these I could cope with as long as they eventually were covered with hair! It had also been agreed by the Marsden that I should have a break from Herceptin for a while; so I gradually began to recover both mentally and physically.

Oddly enough, the writing of this chapter has coincided with the removal of the Christmas decorations. Strange but true. The bareness of the surroundings reflects the contents of this chapter perfectly. It's funny how sometimes life has a way of putting things into context for you. Also during this chapter, my niece Kirsti came back from a night out and asked if she could read my book. It was early hours of the morning so I went to bed and left her to it. When I returned to continue writing, this is what I found:

Tine this is such a beautiful book

I never fully realised how brave and courageous you are until I read all of this. It is so beautiful, I just wanted you to know I am so inspired by you and every day I feel you give me the strength to carry on... I know this is going to sound really cheesey but I love, love, love having you here and staying with us!! You are seriously part of our lives and I know that everyone will agree with me when I say you are one hell of a character and we never want you to change because you bring us a little bit more sun light into this house! I am also going to agree with you on the fact that Mum and Dad are not people but angels, and that they just wanted to stay for the ride! Because they are two of the most beautiful and caring people I have ever known (I am just glad that they are my parents)!!

I know this isnt really my place to say this is but I'm so proud of you Tine you are the only person I know who could face this time with a smile on your face, a glass of wine in your hand and a fag in the other! (Maybe that is not so appropriate but hey, who cares? Live life to its fullest) because if Im honest, every one else would go running for the hills! I just want you to know that the whole family is forever thinking of you, that includes your two because I am always having conversations with Lauren and I think that she is growing up so fast and is going to turn into a beautiful-minded young lady, also Chris is always so thoughtful and is forever talking about you!! Don't ever forget that!

I feel that having you living here has strenthen (sorry I don't know how to spell that) our relationship, you no longer feel like just an auntie but you are now one of my friends. You are so special to me!

All of my love and friendship

Koo
Xxx

P.s. I'm sorry for writing it in your book space but I couldn't find a pen or paper!

She is nearly 17 years old and is the most amazing teenager. She has an affinity with people that is rare to find in someone so young. I could not actually believe what I was reading but was so touched that it reduced me to tears (again! There have been a lot of those since commencing this book!). I felt I had to share this with you to give you an insight into the wonderful family that I have now become part of, and the close bond that exists between us all. Like her mother, Kirsti is also a beautiful person – inside and out – in fact they all are.

PART FOUR

''Cause I have found a dream that must come true,
Every ounce of me must see it through…
I'm sorry I don't have a role for love to play,
Hand over my heart I'll find my way…'

Chapter 10

Medicine Versus Therapy

WHEN I was first diagnosed with breast cancer, it was such a shock that I didn't really know how to deal with it. I'm not a great reader so unlike my sister-in-law Karen, I didn't try and digest as much information about the illness as possible. I read what I needed to (the Marsden provide an excellent leaflet on how to approach the subject with your children, amongst numerous others) but left the maintenance of the disease very much to the professionals as I thought they must know best. I didn't immediately alter my lifestyle or my diet, after all I was relatively fit anyway and would consider my diet at that time to be adequate – maybe a few too many carbohydrates (I do love my puddings and chocolate!), but it was pretty balanced. I am one of those very lucky people who seem to be able to eat what I like without having a weight problem. I have also always smoked, well seriously since I was 16 but I am not a heavy smoker and tend not to inhale deeply. However, I have tried to give up on numerous occasions… unsuccessfully I'm afraid to say.

The only times that it has been successful, was for a brief period when I was pregnant both times, prior to reconstructive surgery, and after the liver cancer but I unfortunately have always gone back to it. At times I have been very hard on myself about this. After all, the doctors are trying everything possible to improve my health so shouldn't I be doing the same? The fact is that a) I enjoy it, and b) I have been told that there is no evidence to suggest that it is associated with breast cancer; lung and throat cancer, yes, but not breast cancer. I know that it would be advisable on general health grounds to quit but at the end of the day, I really don't think it has any bearing on the progression of my disease. Two of the major organs that have not been affected by the disease so far are my heart (although this was affected by the treatment of it (Herceptin)), and lungs. This is not to say though, that the disease will not eventually reach these.

I am certainly not trying to justify the fact that I smoke but I do believe that you have to be true to yourself. This is part of who I am. I can change that but at present I do not feel inclined to do so. In a way it's like a crutch or a friend (not a very good one I hear you say!) but it's something I need at the moment. I gave up for six months last year and then had a brain tumour, which indicated to me – rightly or wrongly – that it made no difference (although maybe it is the cumulative effect over time that we have to consider?). But let's face it, isn't it just a little after the horse has already bolted?! And is there not enough pollution in the air that we breathe anyway? Plus, we all know that people who do not smoke, unfortunately also contract cancer. I wish I could be one of these social smokers but I'm afraid, being an addictive personality, it's all or nothing with me! I keep saying to myself that when my life is fuller and I have less time on my hands I will give up for good – famous last words!

As for alternative therapies, I have tried yoga and in my capacity as a beauty therapist, I have always been aware of the benefits of exercise, diet, relaxation and massage but in my opinion, I am afraid that alternative therapies alone do not cure cancer. If they did, then we would be strongly advised by the professionals to try them, and this is not the case. Conventional medicine is the only thing that works; that is why millions of pounds are spent on researching and patenting treatments and some brilliant minds are utilised in the pursuit of this. Others may dispute this and there is occasionally someone who has rejected conventional treatment to follow a strict diet of just puréed fruit and vegetables and their cancer has miraculously vanished; but I would say that they have just been incredibly lucky – God was obviously smiling down on them. I have known people who have radically changed their diets and other aspects of their lifestyle, a couple of whom are sadly no longer here, whereas thankfully I am. What's more, in the same way as medical treatments, what works for one person, will not necessarily work for the next – we are all so individual.

There is a great deal of literature on the subject but I think it is quite dangerous to rely solely on the experiences of a handful of people; having said that, I am all for complementary therapies. I haven't actually taken advantage of the range of palliative care, or support groups offered by the Marsden, or the many other facilities offered by various cancer charities. I am saving these for when I feel I really need them. I did try a psychotherapy session once when I was at one of my lowest points, but I felt it wasn't for me at the time. I do however, exercise and take vitamins and am not averse to trying anything that may help the treatment to work more effectively. I agree that they can focus the mind and they are certainly beneficial in the area of pain relief and management. They can give you a feeling of general well-being and calm, which in turn has the ability to increase endorphins and thus positivity. So utilising these alongside the standard medication can often be very beneficial. It is the use of them alone that I do not subscribe to.

So how do other people deal with cancer? There have been many celebrities in the tabloids over the last few years, whose illness has been highlighted because of who they are. It must be very difficult being in the public eye and having to go through something as traumatic and personal as this; it's hard enough when you're just Joe Bloggs. They can't hide. Or they can try but the paparazzi are so relentless that this would be extremely difficult for them. I remember being at the doctors once when Kylie had first been diagnosed and my doctor asked me how I felt about this. I said that it just proves how indiscriminate cancer is, and how all the success and money in the world does not give you immunity. Here's a fine example of a supposedly blessed, fit young lady who tragically could not escape cancer's grasp. Like me, she chose bandanas over wigs and I think she looks amazing. I truly admire her courage.

Others obviously include Caron Keating and Marsha Hunt. I followed Caron's progress with great interest and empathy. Another successful, intelligent, attractive young lady, whose talent had made her famous and unfortunately, whose illness has continued her fame. I was touched by the deep love her mother and close family had for her; it reminded me to a certain extent of my own situation. She went to the other side of the world in search of a cure and tried all sorts of alternative therapies. Maybe they prolonged her life, maybe not, but she fought the illness with such bravery and strength, and had such a positive attitude, that she remains a shining example of how one should deal with life threatening illness. I'm sure she has left a huge void in the lives of all who knew her that nothing and nobody else could fill, but her memory lives on.

In fact, I remember Gloria Hunniford (her mother) relaying a story about white feathers, saying that she had come across them in the most unusual situations. These, she interpreted as a sign from Caron. It's strange how certain things stick in your mind as I was in the garden having a cigarette one day, when a white feather came from what appeared to be nowhere and fluttered at my feet. I was going through a particularly rough time then and I automatically said 'Thanks Caron' as if I felt she was trying to give me the strength and belief that I would get through this. Her story had certainly had an effect on me.

Marsha Hunt approached it in an entirely different way. It's almost as if she celebrated it. When she was about to lose her hair, she had a head shaving party and invited close friends and family along to witness it. Fair play to her but I'm sure most of us do not feel like this. She must be a remarkable woman. On the other hand, although she can deal with it in this way, I'm not so sure that those close to her would be celebrating. She said that after the treatment she may actually keep the shaven look! You have to be very confident and self-assured to be able to carry that off. Still she was a model, so she obviously can get away with it, unlike the majority of the rest of us!

I think it is easier at the beginning of the illness to be positive and put on a brave face as there is the possibility of being cured. It is as the illness progresses, and you know you have it for life, that your faith diminishes. However, I wish her and Kylie all the luck in the world and hope that they make a full and swift recovery. Another shining example is Jane Macdonald who has run marathons, overcoming the weakness and pain that cancer has afforded her body, to reach her goal. She has raised a great deal of money and awareness for cancer research. What an outstanding achievement. Again, she has the full support of her family, who appear to have an amazing attitude. I am sure that this makes a difference.

Finally, although Mo Mowlan's illness was not breast cancer but a brain tumour, I can relate to her too. She carried on her duties in the public eye remarkably well. She was a very determined woman who appeared to live life to the full for as long as she could. We obviously have the brain tumour in common and whilst going through my own ordeal, I would visualise pictures of her in the newspaper, bravely carrying on, with her thinning hair and bloatedness due to the steroids. I admired her tenacity and sense of purpose. But one thing that her husband said did worry me. He was adamant that her death was as a direct result of the radiotherapy to her brain, rather than the actual tumour itself.

It did make me wonder whether the treatment of the illness has a more severe effect than we are aware of.

Just like chemo, which is really a poison and obviously affects good blood cells as wells as diseased ones, radiotherapy has a detrimental effect to the body. And, as I have already mentioned, although Herceptin is being hailed as the new 'wonder drug' and some people are fighting to get it, it can cause serious heart problems in a small proportion of people. In any case it is only effective for those patients whose breast cancer 'over-expresses' the Her-2 protein (about 20% of breast cancers). In the UK it can be prescribed for any patient with secondary or metastatic breast cancer which is Her-2 positive. Recent trials have also shown that if it is given after surgery for primary cancer of this type, it can reduce the risk of the cancer coming back by about 50% compared with chemo alone.

However it is incredibly expensive, which is why it is not offered to everybody in the latter category. I investigated the cost of it when I was planning to return to Spain and to give you some idea, the Marsden quoted me approximately £500 per vial, in comparison to £165 for Pamidronate (or Bonefos in tablet form), which is the other drug I take, used to strengthen the bones of those with bone cancer; and this is the cost of the drug alone, it does not take into account the added costs of the cannulas, nurses etc. But I suppose a potent illness demands an equally potent, and therefore costly, treatment and where would we be without it?

Aside from celebrities, there are many, many ordinary people living with cancer in the UK and worldwide. And just because they are not in the public eye, does not mean that they are not equally as amazing and courageous – it's just that we do not see or hear of them. They do walks and hold other events to raise money for cancer research, and without them, we wouldn't be where we are today. Cancer touches the lives of so many families, who all, in their own right, are fighting the disease with everything they've got, and doing what they can to support the various charities. I myself have donated money and last year did the ten-mile Ashtead Twilight Walk with my sister and some of her friends in aid of The Breakthrough Cancer Trust. You just feel that after all the brilliant and, at times, very expensive treatment you have received, you want to give something back.

I also did some filming for the Marsden that I hope was of benefit to other cancer sufferers. I never actually saw it myself as it was shown on a TV channel that I don't possess (I also didn't particularly want to watch myself having chemo and see someone I didn't recognise staring back at me!). When I was first asked, I assumed that it was just going to be filming of the ward generally, but it turned out to be very one-to-one. I surprisingly, wasn't at all nervous but I felt really sorry for the nurse working with me as, as I have previously mentioned, I have very difficult veins at the best of times and due to her nerves, it took six attempts to get the cannula in! This meant that it took much longer than I think the film crew anticipated. Still, we got there in the end! I hope it achieved the desired effect, and I also hope that this book goes further to helping the cause.

You see, whenever I go to the Marsden and see someone young, or a child with cancer, it upsets me. On one occasion, there was a child on a trolley who was obviously very poorly, accompanied by his young mother who was in tears; the vision still haunts me.

And another time, waiting for a scan, there was an even younger mother sitting in a wheelchair cradling her toddler son. At first I thought it was the mother who was ill, until I noticed the tubes coming from the child. At other times there have been people whose skin is severely jaundiced as a result of liver cancer; those with unusually distended stomachs and some who are so incredibly thin that it is a wonder they can walk unsupported. But it is the children who get me every time. As a parent, I find it inconceivable that any parent could possibly come to terms with that. You would so want to swap places with the child; it must be the most heart-breaking thing that any parent could ever endure. It's at times like these that I question whether there is a god; religious people however, may argue that this is the devil's work.

So is cancer caused by external influences, or is it genetic? We are still not really any further on with this debate although it is generally thought that it is probably a combination of both. Having said that, although there has been a great deal of cancer in my own family, out of 6 cases only 1 has been cancer of the breast; the rest included bone, thyroid, throat, lung and leukaemia; and the one incidence of breast cancer was in someone much older. My personal theory on this is that it may lie dormant in some people and need a trigger, like stress or hormone imbalance, to start it off. I, unfortunately had both, but that doesn't make my cancer any worse, or better for that matter, than anybody else's. It is very dependent on the aggressiveness of the tumour, it would seem. In any case, it is sometimes so far advanced that it is perhaps not always possible to determine the source.

Another issue is whether delaying having children and not breast feeding them has an effect. There does seem to be some correlation between the incidence of breast cancer and mothers who have left child bearing until later in life. I was 30 when I had my first child and whilst I loved the closeness and the bonding that breast feeding afforded, I was unable to continue after a few months as I just did not seem to produce enough milk to keep my baby satisfied for long. This meant that I either had a baby continually hanging from my breasts (which made them very sore), or I had an unsettled baby who would not sleep, which made life exhausting. My mother did not breast feed either Kim or myself, yet my sister thankfully is extremely healthy; she incidentally, breastfed all four of her children, and Beth, her youngest, for a significantly long period.

Whether these factors are relevant or not, I don't know; but I am just grateful that my cancer was detected before it was too late and that I've been lucky enough to have had 6 more years of life so far. I thank the Marsden mainly for this. Their care has been second to none; the staff are fantastic, the treatments are the latest available and the atmosphere and attitude is one of calm and caring. I think you have to be a very special type of person to work there. I cannot praise them enough.

Chapter 11

Dreams & Aspirations

I HAVE always been one of those people who has difficulty sticking at things, I get bored so easily. In fact the only thing that I did stick at was my HND; but even that was a bit 'hit and miss' towards the end, although I did succeed and actually did very well. I dropped out of my 'A' levels and many jobs because I was bored, yet I really didn't know what it was that I wanted to do. My parents would vouch for that; we used to have endless discussions on the subject but we never quite reached a conclusion.

I do now wonder whether it was not just due to boredom though, but depression. Ever since puberty I have had a problem with my hormones, I was terribly premenstrual and during my teens, a complete nightmare to live with! I was rebellious and quite selfish at times although by nature, I would consider myself to be a kind-hearted person. There was the post-natal depression and various other bouts throughout my life that would indicate a depressive tendency – even Mark said he had never met anyone who suffered with their hormones so much. I was also totally incapable of making a decision and sticking to it; everyone else used to make them for me. My life has therefore been directionless thus far so I am determined now to correct that and take control.

As I mentioned earlier, I have always had the ambition to write a book. I would consider English to be one of my fortes. (I always used to get very high marks in my essays at college). And now that I had so much material to work with, this seemed like the ideal opportunity to fulfil this ambition. I want to see it through; not just for my sake but for my family's too. To do so at this stage of my life and in these circumstances, I feel would be a great achievement; and not just a personal one. I so want to give something back and hopefully to help others going through a similar experience. If this book in any way achieves that, then it will be a success in my eyes; regardless of whether it sells well or not, I will have achieved what I set out to do. (Having said that, I hope that it does sell as I would very much like to donate some of the proceeds to cancer research; so the more I do sell, the better for the charity).

Since the brain tumour I have not endeavoured to seek a relationship as there are so many other factors that I need to address before that. Obviously, first and foremost I need to make sure that my health situation is stable. There is no point embarking on a new relationship if this is not the case; that would be too much to ask of anyone… and myself. I have sufficed with seeing close friends and although I miss the intimacy of a loving relationship, and it has been very difficult going through the later stages of the illness alone, that was my choice and in a way I feel it was the right one.

It has certainly given me the time to ascertain what it is

I don't want, even if I haven't actually established what I do want yet! At times I have felt like I wasted the best years of my life being in the wrong relationship for so long, and not fulfilling any of my own personal ambitions. After all, what is the point in having dreams if you don't strive to achieve them? But actually, I didn't entirely know what they were until now. With maturity, comes a self-assururance that you sometimes lack in youth. I had some very happy times with Mark and we produced 2 beautiful children; but I was not completely myself, I felt restrained in some way.

The love I had for him was almost like a brotherly love. When we first split up I did everything I could to make it a little easier for him; I even suggested that if he wanted to see the children more regularly, he could come back and live at the house. I would've made the dining room into his room so that he could have some privacy if he needed it. I would not even have objected to him entertaining his friends – why should I, it was his home too. When the tables were turned though and I needed some help, or just someone to talk to, he was not there for me in the same way. It made me realise just how complex relationships are, and how one person's strength is another's weakness. I learnt a lot during that time though, so how can that possibly be a waste? After all, isn't that what we're here for?

Long term illness has such a profound effect on all aspects of your life – it certainly affects your thought processes as I think I have clearly demonstrated! Maybe I did lose the plot for a while but when panic sets in, you are prone to do some very rash things. Who knows, if I hadn't had cancer would I have left Mark? Would I have experienced all the emotions and expressed all the love that I have? Would I ever have written this book? It's doubtful and yet I feel I have lost so much. But I have also gained. I hope I am a better person for all of this, that I have contributed something to peoples' lives and that ultimately I will be remembered for my good traits and not my bad. We all have faults of course; we wouldn't be human if we didn't.

I am medically at the stage now, where I have just the couple of small lumps in my neck and no further cancer elsewhere. They cannot cure this but they can control it. I am currently on a course of tablet-form chemo called Capecitabine, which incidentally, was the treatment I took myself off for Christmas. It again has side effects, among which are lethargy, anorexia (loss of appetite), diarrhoea, altered taste, mouth ulcers, infections and palmar-plantar erythema. Of which I have experienced some in varying degrees, particularly the latter, which basically means that the hands and feet go a strange red/purple colour in places, and the skins dries and peels off. In my case, it also gave me a burning sensation in the feet on more than one occasion. So you can see why I decided to have a break while my children were here! However, if it is doing the job it was designed for, then I'm sure I can cope with the side effects. At least this time, there is no hair loss. Yippee!

In fact my hair is doing very nicely now, not a bald patch in sight! So it's time to get back on with my life. But where do I want it to go and what do I want to do? First and foremost, I want to ensure that I stay as healthy as possible during this course of treatment, which I think I am achieving. Lots of exercise (I do a half hour Stretch and

Tone DVD every week day), balanced diet, vitamins, especially vitamin C – due to the smoking – minimal cigarettes, and above all a positive attitude. Once I have finished this book, which is fairly imminent, I am going to have even more time on my hands. Time to get a proper job! I have thought long and hard about what I would like to do. A career, I feel is probably out of the question for the immediate future, but I do need to get out of the house amongst people. Writing this book has been like therapy for me, but it is a very lonely pursuit.

I can be quite a sociable person in the right circumstances, although when I am low I do tend to withdraw; but generally in a work environment, I can get along with most people. I also feel like I need a light-hearted atmosphere, nothing too serious. So it struck me that a bar job might be ideal at the moment. This type of position tends to be fairly casual too, which would suit me. Part-time I feel would be preferable to start with, to see how my health holds up. The only thing is, it will have to be local; the no driving thing, remember? In fact the six months was up in November and I did reapply, only to be told that I had originally been given the wrong information; the standard time, set by the General Medical Council is two years. I could appeal but this may cost me a great deal of money in solicitor's fees, only to achieve the same outcome, so what would be the point of that? However, it didn't stop me being bitterly disappointed when the brown envelope from the DVLA came though the door.

The other thing I need to address is housing. I have been offered only 1 council property, even though I have been on the list for over 2 years. They have also changed the banding system this year; whereas before Christmas I was a high priority, I am now in Band C (A being the highest and E the lowest) so this is not looking promising. The one property I did get offered was in a terrible state. I did go and view it with my sister and parents; lovely location but totally impractical without a car. And the décor, if you can call it that, left a lot to be desired (there were five different pieces of carpet in the bedroom alone!). The bath however was in pristine condition; in fact it looked like it had never actually been used! Beyond all this, there would have been possible potential if the lounge had not been so tiny; let's just say it would have been crowded with myself and the 2 children in it! And the bedroom unfortunately overlooked a very run down garden belonging to the tenant downstairs, rather than your own. Needless to say, I didn't take it!

Do you know one of my favourite pastimes is sleeping? I have always loved my bed, particularly in the winter when it's cold and dark. It's by contrast so warm and cosy. Many people would say 'what a waste of time' but when your life is the nightmare, it's easy to escape into sleep and relish your dreams; especially when you have little to get up for. To live them, even if it is only in your subconscious, is some compensation when you know you may not be able to do it in reality. My bed is my haven. At times, I have wished I didn't wake up at all. But then I challenge myself: either I can lay here and wait to die, or do something constructive and worthwhile – something to be remembered by. It only takes one look at the photo of my children by my bedside and I'm up (eventually!), ready for another tirade of obstacles to come my way.

I take my cocktail of tablets and rattle all the way to

my next task! It's strange but you suddenly become preoccupied with things like wills and funeral details… just in case. I wanted to make sure that my family would know my wishes if the worst came to the worst; including what my instructions would be if I had a further brain tumour and was left in a vegetative state. There is no way that I would want to be kept alive by machines, or become a further burden on them so my instructions are very clear: turn off any machine that is keeping me alive and retire me to a hospice if the cancer becomes too much to cope with; that is what they are there for. As for my funeral, I would obviously have to have 'Immortality' played but Eva Cassidy's 'Somewhere Over the Rainbow' is another favourite as this is ultimately what I am looking for, my pot of gold at the end of it. Unfortunately I cannot donate my organs, which is something I would have considered if I didn't have cancer.

On to brighter things, what other dreams and aspirations do I have? Many, but the ultimate dream is obviously to be well. None of the others can be achieved without this. I do not necessarily mean free of cancer (although that would be nice!), I just mean well enough to have a good quality of life; to enjoy life. What I have learnt through this experience is that you should always take up on opportunities. If you do, your life can take a completely different course, if you don't, you will never know. I do not want to have any more regrets and there have been far too many missed opportunities in the past. I have also suffered at the hands of my own harsh treatment. It's time to forgive myself, to move on, to become the successful, appealing person that I aspire to be.

But how to do this? As I have said, having secondary cancer eventually strips you of everything. It has now become almost like a game but cancer is winning hands down at the moment. I have got to start from scratch in every department and at 42 years of age, this is going to be no mean feat! I think just to get out there would be a good place to begin. Things tend to happen once you do this, doors open. One step at a time though. It needs to be a gradual process; I can't expect it all to happen at once (which is something I always used to do). The ultimate aim is to slowly get back all that I have lost… bit by bit. The hair was a good start; perhaps this will help with my confidence and self-esteem. But my main dreams are still to have my breast reconstructed – to be whole again – and to acquire a home, which will adequately accommodate my children; the other things will be reclaimed in time, and who knows? Maybe even love will follow.

Chapter 12

Hope & Happiness

AS I mentioned in the previous chapter, I have recently realised the importance of taking up on opportunities and have already started to put this into action. Earlier last year the Marsden contacted me out of the blue, and told me that someone had very kindly donated 2 tickets to Live8 and would I be interested? They wanted to give them to someone who would appreciate them and the nurses had selected little old me! I couldn't quite believe my luck as things like that rarely happen to me. Normally I would have turned them down, thinking I wasn't deserving of them, and told them to give them to someone else; but this time I thought 'it's a once in a lifetime opportunity and why shouldn't I accept? They obviously thought I was worthy so maybe I should think the same.' So I did. But the next problem was who to take with me. There were so many people I wanted to thank but in the end, there was only really one obvious choice – my daughter, Lauren.

You see, I had always wanted to take Lauren to a concert. In fact when she was younger I had booked for us to go to one of the 'X Factor' concerts as we have both always been fans. Unfortunately, they were not able to fill the venue and it was cancelled, which was very disappointing, so I felt this would more than make up for it – it was the grandaddy of all concerts after all! It would also enable us to spend some time together, just the two of us. (I had decided that I would do something solely for Christopher at a later date).

So I told Lauren, who had to cancel a former engagement as it was quite short notice, and on July 2nd 2005 we made our way to Hyde Park. Although we had arrived in ample time, the queues were unbelievable – I think it took us an hour and a half just to get to the entrance, but it was well worth the wait. Once inside, Lauren found a large screen and decided we should stay in this spot; but my feeling was that if you were just going to watch it on a screen, you might as well have stayed at home and watched it on TV.

I wanted to absorb the atmosphere of the occasion, so we edged through the crowds as far forward as we could and ended up just behind the golden circle. Although we were in sight of the stage, the artists still appeared like little specks in the distance but fortunately we had a screen just to our right so we weren't in danger of missing anything (or so we thought). The magnitude of the event was overwhelming. Lauren, I think, hadn't known quite what to expect, having never been to a concert before, and at first she was a little unsure, mainly due to the volume of people and the fact that there was no seating except for the ground! However, she soon got into the swing of things and was swept up in the excitement and emotion of the occasion like everyone else. We were dancing away with the rest of them and someone gave Lauren a huge inflatable microphone that she kept as a souvenir.

It was a fantastic, if long day. But unfortunately because it over-ran, we had to leave before the end to get our train home. Lauren had had enough anyway, she was tired and needed her bed but it meant that we missed some of our favourite artists. We were hanging on and hanging on hoping to see Lauren's favourite Mariah Carey but she was just on too late, and we didn't even get the opportunity of seeing her on TV as we were on the train home during her performance. Still, I was sure they would bring out a DVD of the concert so I knew that we would get the opportunity to see the rest at a later date. (My sister and brother-in-law very kindly bought it for me for Christmas so we have now seen what we missed and relived the rest!). It was brilliant to be able to share this experience with my daughter and I vowed from that day that I would find more special things to do with the children and my family. That is what life should be about.

Next on the agenda was to belatedly celebrate my and Jenny's birthdays. I had been ill on both occasions but was determined that we should do something to add to our special times. We decided to go up to London and see a show. First stop though was a spot of lunch. We found this really nice little wine bar and I surprised Jen by ordering a bottle of champagne. After all, if you're going to celebrate, you might as well do it in style! So we consumed this with a lovely lunch, followed by a couple of cocktails. Jen said she felt like a 'posh bird' all day! We then went off to see the Oxford Street Christmas lights being switched on. Some of the 'X Factor' contestants, as well as Westlife, were there and Jen and I were dancing in the street like a couple of maniacs after all that alcohol! It was great fun, despite the odd looks we were getting from the more staid members of the audience (no one could ever accuse us of being that!). We then went on to the show. It was another fantastic day.

While we were walking up Oxford Street, we were stopped by a lady selling something. Normally I would just walk on by and say 'no thank you' but this time I didn't. She turned out to be an actress/photographer and was looking for people to attend The Studio (as seen on TV!). It was such a good deal that I couldn't turn it down so I bought the voucher, which again is something I have never done in my life before! It's basically a pampering day, but you also get a free magazine-style photo shoot and a free print included in the package. The first part of the offer was for 2 people so I had the dilemma of who to take again. Jen isn't really into this type of thing so the obvious choice for this was my sister, who very definitely is (well, the pampering part at least – not so sure about the photo shoot!). I also get a free haircut at a top salon in Mayfair so when I need my first haircut since it has grown back, I will be going there for it. The Studio Day is scheduled for 8th February and we're both really looking forward to it. That's what I mean about taking up on opportunities. If you don't, you'll never know what you might've missed.

Another example that springs to mind is a while ago, when I was away at Butlins with Sharon, we came across a recording studio in the grounds. Sharon, having a very good voice, wanted to record a CD. So we spent an hour or so one afternoon doing this. Another carer and I went into the studio with her and became her dance troupe while she performed! It was really good fun and the CD turned out great. My daughter also has a very good voice and I sing a little too so Lauren decided that she would like to make a CD with me. We are therefore going to Butlins at half-term with my parents and this will certainly be on the 'to do list'! That would be something really special for us both to have as a keepsake and who knows, it may be the first of many for Lauren.

Chris is also coming – obviously – and I really must sort something out for me and him to share. I did look into taking him to a Premier Division football match but the tickets were horrendously expensive. Still, occasionally you hear of a special offer so I'm hoping that this will happen this year. I have also recently received a letter from the Plastic Surgery department of the Marsden to attend clinic in March, and this has given me the incentive to give up smoking again. They will not perform the reconstructive surgery if you smoke and I want this so much. I also owe it to my children to try. Things appear to be looking up! Maybe 2006 will be my year.

So you see I have finally realised that I deserve some happiness and the kids deserve some treats after everything we have all been through. No more beating myself up; what's done is done and I can't change it. 'It's all in the past now' as my husband would say. Time to look to the future, whatever that may hold. Today is the beginning of the rest of my life, and life is a precious gift so we should all try and make the most of it. One thing I will endeavour to do is to be vigilant of, and protect my children. Breast cancer is on both sides of the family, and there has been a great deal of cancer-related illness on my side so I must ensure that Lauren, particularly, is screened at the earliest possible time. I also want to ensure that if they are experiencing problems as a result of everything they have had to endure, we address these sooner rather than later. I want them to be as happy and well-adjusted as it is possible for them to be in the circumstances.

I truly hope that I have proved that there is life after a diagnosis of cancer. It's not always easy and you have to adjust to all the changes that occur during the illness but 6 years on and I'm still here! It's a very different type of life and at times, it has just felt like an existence; but there are still good times to be had, and in fact you appreciate these even more. No more taking things for granted. As I have said before: 'where there's life, there's hope'. The medical profession are finding new and better treatments all the time and who knows how far we are from a cure? That is ultimately what I hope for. Not just for myself, but for all cancer sufferers. Wouldn't that be great? No barriers to stop them reaching their potential and fulfilling their dreams. I still see myself in a little villa in Spain, basking in the sunshine and drinking Sangria, with men ogling my new pert breasts (while their partners give them a big hard dig with their elbow!). Well, I can dream, can't I?!

What I would say to you is that I have learnt some invaluable lessons through all of this: the first is that it is imperative to know your own body, and take control on occasions. Don't be afraid to voice your opinions. If you are experiencing discomfort, or are convinced that you have a problem in a certain area, get it checked out. Doctors are guided by you; you often have to present with symptoms before they are able to help you. I have experienced this with both the illness and the treatment of it, and fortunately for me, I have had the problem acknowledged and dealt with in time (for the most part). Do what you can to help yourself. I am just an ordinary person going through a not particularly extraordinary ordeal; I am not a celebrity, I am just me and I certainly don't profess to have all the answers, but that is precisely the point! If I can achieve what I have thus far, then so can you.

The second lesson that I have learnt is that it is very important to realise and appreciate what you have – the grass isn't always greener on the other side; it may appear to be at first but it can become very parched and barren before long. You often don't realise what you have right under your nose, or how lucky you are. In my case it's all about quality not quantity of life you see; my cancer is being controlled but I have no idea how long I have left and I so need to love and be loved. I can no longer rely on my appearance alone to attract people; they will have to love me for who I am (which is how it should be and how it was with Mark although it has taken me a long time to appreciate this). It's important to have a partner for support and to share things with – life can be very lonely otherwise. My looks may alter from time to time in line with the disease; it is therefore going to have to be a very caring and understanding individual prepared to take that on. I am sure there is someone out there for me somewhere; it's just a question of finding him and I am forever hopeful!

Finally, and most importantly, it is essential to feel that you belong; your family is the most precious thing you possess, so cherish yours. I don't think I'd be here today if it wasn't for mine. When you receive text messages like this from your daughter and niece, it really puts things in perspective and makes you want to protect their future even more:

> 'Mum, I miss u x x x. Course I will always tell u everything luv u x x x x x x x x'

and

> 'Hi tine sorry its late but I read ur book+I want u2no ur a truly amazing woman how u've done it I don't know! But we all have so much admiration 4u!Love hannie Xx'.

There has been many a kind word spoken during my illness but when it hails from the young, it seems to pull at your heart strings so intensely that you want to ensure that they never have to experience what you have had to endure. This also endorses the fact that I have not lost my children, they are still very much a huge part of my life and I love them so much it hurts.

And whilst I have lost friends and family to cancer and know many more battling it, I think that maybe those we have lost have gone to a better place. But I am not quite ready to join them. I truly believe that there is something after this life and that we will meet our loved ones again – maybe not in the form that we know them now but to quote a line from a famous film 'I'll see you again… but not yet!' And as Robbie Williams says in his song 'There is no dignity in death'; life carries on regardless and dying is abhorrent however it occurs. I therefore want to do everything in my power to make a difference while I still can, and to enjoy and nurture the relationships that I share with the special people in my life. Maybe I'll even be able to add to this collection. There can be a light at the end of the tunnel, even if it is only faintly glimmering; none of us know what is around the corner but whatever happens, I intend to fight every inch of the way and I sincerely hope that if you are in a similar position, I have inspired you to do the same…

'Immortality
There is a vision and a fire in me
I keep the memory of you and me, inside
And we don't say goodbye
We don't say goodbye
With all my love for you
And what else we may do
We don't say, goodbye.'